Published by Pedigree in association with the **Daily Mirror**
Pedigree Books Limited, Beech House, Walnut Gardens, Exeter, Devon, EX4 4DH.
www.pedigreebooks.com
email:**books@pedigreegroup.co.uk**
Pedigree trademark, email and website addresses are the sole and exclusive
properties of Pedigree Group Limited, used under license in this publication.

Andy Capp™ can be enjoyed every day in the **Daily Mirror** newspaper or online at
Mirror.co.uk

Andy Capp™ 2015 Yearbook created by
Sean Garnett
Lawrence Goldsmith
Simon Flavin
Fergus McKenna

Designed by
Paul Futcher

Managing Editor: Eugene Duffy, Mirrorpix: Fergus McKenna, Simon Flavin,
David Scripps, Vito Inglese and Paul Mason, Sub-Editor: Hanna Tavner

With thanks to
The editorial team of **Andy Capp™** - Roger Mahoney, Lawrence Goldsmith and
Sean Garnett and the late and great Reg Smythe the original creator of
Andy Capp™. Also to George Rankin of The Content Bureau for supplying the
puzzles, quizzes and crosswords.

All dates of the listed sporting events were correct at the time of going to press.

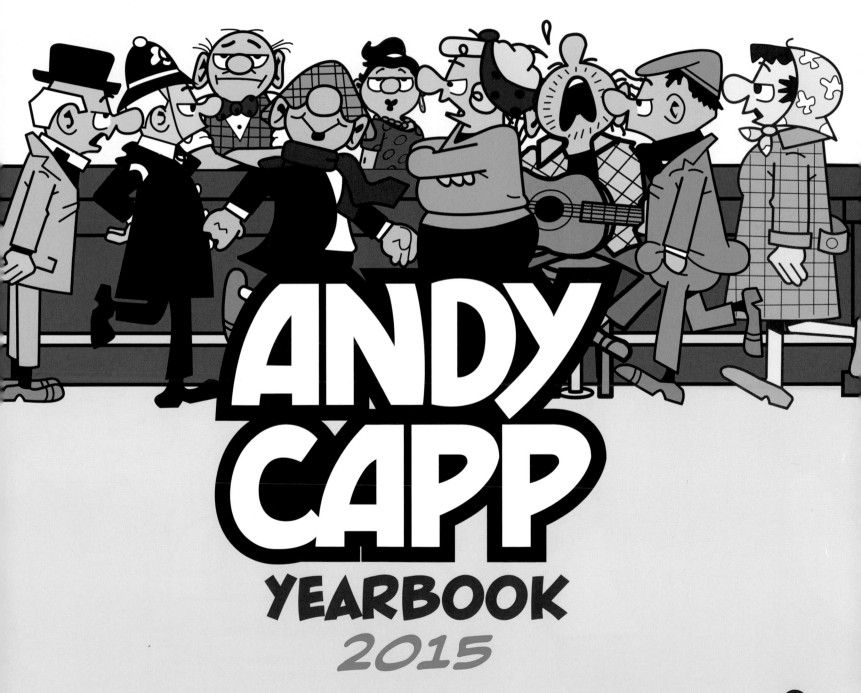

In my bumper yearbook, we'll be taking a trip down memory lane with a look at some of my hilarious antics with Flo, Chalkie, Ruby and the others over the past couple of years.

You're also in fer a proper treat as I share the benefit of my vast, and often underrated, experience to give you tips on a range of stuff from getting fit after Christmas and chatting up lasses (a bit of a speciality of mine, I think you'll agree) to having a flutter on the nags and fishing.

Flo will be providing some recipes for delicious dishes but, luckily fer you, she won't be cooking them, ha ha.. only joking, pet.

And good old Chalkie's even got in on the act with a load of top class gags that will have you doubled up with laughter (he bought me a couple of pints to write that last bit).

You'll also be hearing from the vicar and Guitar Bob – although, not too loudly, I hope for the sake of your ears.

And my favourite barman Jack is going to scramble your brains with a few pub quizzes so you and yer mates can see who's the daftest.

So, sit back, pour yersels a beer – don't forget mine, a packet of crisps would be nice, too – and prepare for a barrel of laughs...

JANUARY

THURSDAY

1

New Year's Day

FRIDAY

2

Bank Holiday (Scotland)

SATURDAY

3

SUNDAY

4

MONDAY

5

TUESDAY

6

WEDNESDAY

7

THURSDAY

8

FRIDAY

9

SATURDAY

10

SUNDAY

11

MONDAY

12

TUESDAY

13

WEDNESDAY

14

THURSDAY

15

FRIDAY

16

THINGS TO DO

SATURDAY **17**	SUNDAY **25**
SUNDAY **18**	MONDAY **26**
MONDAY **19**	TUESDAY **27**
TUESDAY **20**	WEDNESDAY **28**
WEDNESDAY **21**	THURSDAY **29**
THURSDAY **22**	FRIDAY **30**
FRIDAY **23**	SATURDAY **31**
SATURDAY **24**	

THINGS TO DO

SPORTING EVENTS TO KEEP AN EYE OUT FOR
FA Cup Third Round – 3rd January to 4th January
Snooker – The Masters – 11th January to 18th January
Football – African Cup of Nations – 17 January to 8 February
Tennis – Australian Open – 19th January to 1st February

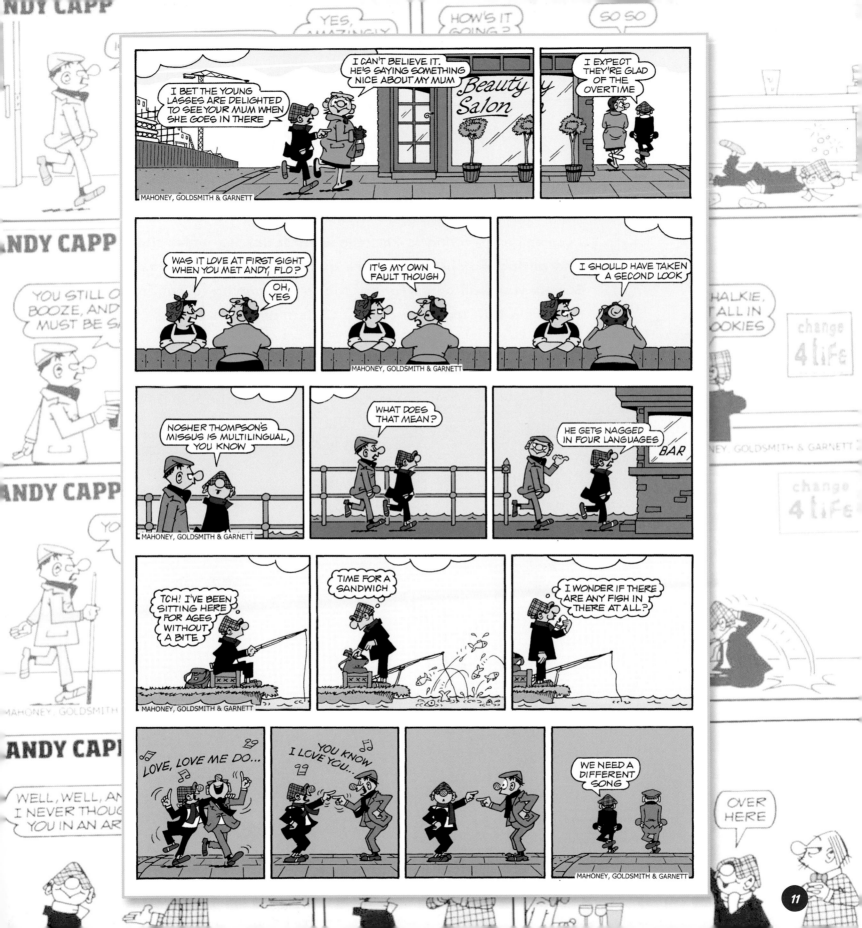

ANDY'S GUIDE TO NEW YEAR FITNESS

Well, what a festive period that was — or so I'm told. The last thing I remember is trying to kiss those three lasses under the mistletoe who all looked alike and spoke at the same time. The rest is a blur. S'pose you'll all be suffering, too, and planning to get fit like me. So here's how to shake off the Christmas excesses...

GO TO A PUB FURTHER AWAY
Apart from the walk, you'll get to meet new friends (more people to buy you drinks).

AND HE OFTEN GETS A RUN IN ON THE WAY HOME WHEN PC BRAITHWAITE CHASES HIM FOR ONE REASON OR ANOTHER.

SOFA EXERCISES
Sounds daft, I know, but when the missus asks you to lift your legs so she can vacuum, leave them up for a little longer. Very good for the muscles.

YOU COULD GET MORE BLINKIN' EXERCISE TAKING THESE EMPTIES OFF THE FLOOR AND TO THE BIN INSTEAD OF LEAVING IT TO ME.

WATCH FOOTBALL ON TELLY
All that leaping off the sofa and jumping up and down when your team scores is good exercise.

And if the useless flamin' lumps lose, you'll burn calories by shaking your fist at the screen and storming off to the pub.

PLAY DARTS, POOL, SNOOKER AND CARDS
Them flamin' know-all docs might scoff at this, but pub sports are still exercise. All that repetitive arm movement must be good for you.

CYCLING

I borrowed Jack's bike once to get home from the pub. That made me feel invigorated, until I had a little mishap at the canal where the bike ride turned into a quick swim.

HE HAD THE CHEEK TO BLAME MY BLOOMIN' BIKE COS THE FRONT BRAKE WAS A BIT SHARP.

BRISK WALKS

An ideal way to lose weight and get the joints moving. Just last night me 'n' Chalkie did about a mile, taking in the Pig and Ferret, the Riveters Arms, the Boilermen's and the new club in the high street.

YES, ALL THAT "WALKING" MADE THEM VERY TIRED... I FOUND THEM ASLEEP IN THE FACTORY LOADING BAY AT 2AM.

CUT DOWN ON FOOD

After all that turkey 'n' stuff you've probably put on a few pounds. Try skipping meals and snack instead. I often miss meals (don't tell Flo, it's because of her cooking).

HE'D PROBABLY ONLY FALL IN THE CANAL AGAIN ANYWAY

GO JOGGING

I've seen Chalkie do this loads of times and he looks and feels better after just a few days. Of course, I'd go with the fella but I don't wanna show him up. And I'm a bit embarrassed by his headband.

GARDENING

A gentle way to loosen those limbs. I often watch Flo through the window pulling up weeds, mowing the lawn and pruning things. Judging by how red she is afterwards, it must be great exercise.

MORE LIKE THEY WOULDN'T BE ABLE TO GET ON WITH THEIR WORKOUTS FOR LAUGHING SO MUCH AT THE SIGHT OF HIM IN A GYM KIT.

JOIN A GYM

The obvious way to get fit. I don't go meself, like, but only cos I'd distract all those lasses with my toned body and rippling muscles.

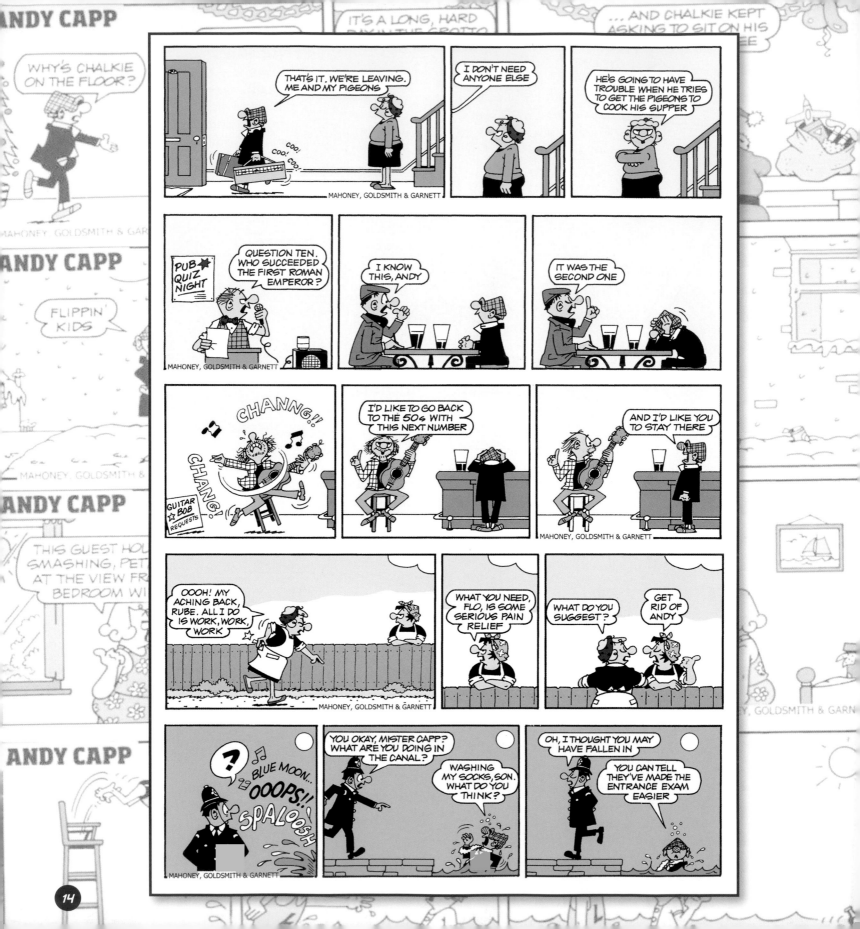

CHALKIE'S CHUCKLES

A man at the airline counter tells the airline rep: "I'd like this bag to go to Berlin, this one to California and this one to London."
The rep says: "I'm sorry sir. We can't do that."
The man replied: "Nonsense. That is what you did last time I flew with you."

Police arrested two kids yesterday, one was drinking battery acid, the other was eating fireworks. They charged one and let the other one off.

Mike, a drunk, staggered into a bar and, after staring for some time at the only woman seated there, walked up to her and gave her a kiss. She jumped up and slapped him really hard. Mike immediately apologised and explained: "Look, I'm sorry. I thought you were my wife. You look exactly like her."
"Why you worthless, insufferable, wretched, no good drunk!" she bellowed at the top of her voice. "Funny," Mike muttered, shaking his head. "You even sound exactly like her."

Two cannibals were eating together. The first says, "Man, I hate my mother-in-law."
The second replies, "So try the potatoes."

A penguin walks into a bar and says: "You seen my brother?"
The barman says: "What's he look like?"

Two nuns are driving through Transylvania when a vampire jumps on the bonnet of their car.
Nun 1: "Turn on the windscreen wipers"
But to no avail! The vampire holds on tightly!
Nun 1 remembers her training and says: "Quick! Show him your cross!"
Nun 2: "GET OFF OF OUR BLOODY CAR!!!"

A man goes to the doctor and says: "Doctor, there's a piece of lettuce sticking out of my bottom." The doctor asks him to drop his trousers and examines him.
The man asks: "Is it serious, doctor?" and the doctor replies: "I'm sorry to tell you, but this is just the tip of the iceberg."

OPENING TIME DISASTER

ANDY'S MANAGED TO GET LOST IN AN UNFAMILIAR PART OF TOWN.

CAN YOU GET HIM THROUGH THE ALLEY TO THE PUB BEFORE JACK GIVES HIS PINT AWAY?

LOOK BACK WITH ANDY

Everybody usually remembers where they were when major events occurred but, for some reason, Andy's memory is a bit hazy!! So, to remind him, here are a few classic Andy strips from some famous dates in history...

Daily Mirror

The time: 9.18 pm, July 20, AD 1969

5d. Monday, July 21, 1969 No. 20,393

MAN ON THE MOON

UNITED STATES

The last practice run

THIS was how the astronauts prepared for the great Moon walk . . . by practising the whole operation inside a Moon simulator at Houston. On the last test run, when this picture was taken, Edwin Aldrin (left) used a scoop for collecting samples while Neil Armstrong tested a camera. Today they know if the rehearsal matched the reality.

AND THE MESSAGE FROM EARTH: WE'RE BREATHING AGAIN!

Man has landed on the Moon. A new era in his history began at 9.18 last night when the lunar module Eagle settled gently on the dusty surface of the Sea of Tranquillity. Inside it—Astronauts Armstrong and Aldrin, destined now for a permanent place in history. They immediately began to prepare for their Moon walk. There are still great perils ahead. But these are truly great achievements. America, the land of frontiersmen, has opened up a new frontier.

FULL STORY—SEE BACK PAGE: THE PATHFINDERS—CENTRE PAGES

ASTRONAUT NEIL ARMSTRONG WALKS ON THE MOON
Issue: 21 July, 1969

DAILY Mirror — The Royal Wedding — CHARLES & DIANA

THE NORTH'S BIGGEST DAILY SALE

(Eire 16p) Thursday, July 30, 1981 ★★★ No. 24,092 12p

SOUVENIR ISSUE

This is the remembered kiss of a Princess in love on a Palace's balcony of kings.

Picture: ALISDAIR MACDONALD

My Princess!

PRINCE CHARLES AND DIANA MARRY
Issue: 30 July, 1981

THE WORD OF CAPP

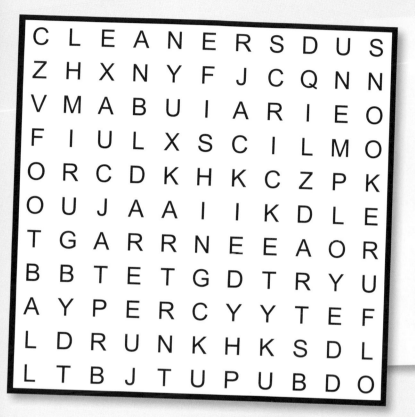

```
C L E A N E R S D U S
Z H X N Y F J C Q N N
V M A B U I A R I E O
F I U L X S C I L M O
O R C D K H K C Z P K
O U J A A I I K D L E
T G A R R N E E A O R
B B T E T G D T R Y U
A Y P E R C Y Y T E F
L D R U N K H K S D L
L T B J T U P U B D O
```

WORD SEARCH

Think you know your Andy Capp characters? How many can you find?

ANDY	**FISHING**	**RUBY**
CHALKIE	**FLO**	**RUGBY**
CLEANER	**FOOTBALL**	**SNOOKER**
CRICKET	**JACKIE**	**UNEMPLOYED**
DARTS	**PERCY**	**VICAR**
DRUNK	**PUB**	

FEBRUARY

SUNDAY

1

MONDAY

2

TUESDAY

3

WEDNESDAY

4

THURSDAY

5

FRIDAY

6

SATURDAY

7

SUNDAY

8

MONDAY

9

TUESDAY

10

WEDNESDAY

11

THURSDAY

12

FRIDAY

13

SATURDAY

14

SUNDAY

15

MONDAY

16

THINGS TO DO

TUESDAY

17

WEDNESDAY

18

THURSDAY

19

FRIDAY

20

SATURDAY

21

SUNDAY

22

MONDAY

23

TUESDAY

24

WEDNESDAY

25

THURSDAY

26

FRIDAY

27

SATURDAY

28

SPORTING EVENTS TO KEEP AN EYE OUT FOR
American Football – Super Bowl XLIX – 1st February
Rugby Union – Six Nations Championship –
6th February – 21st March
Cricket – ICC Cricket World Cup – 14th February –
29th March

THINGS
TO DO

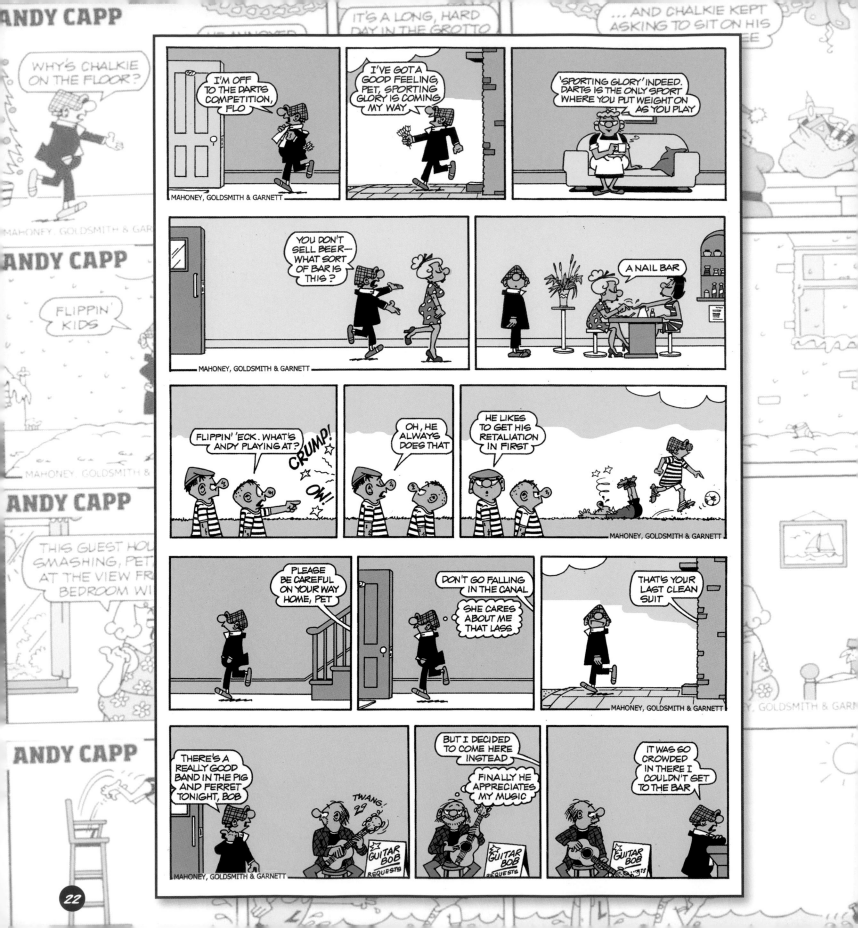

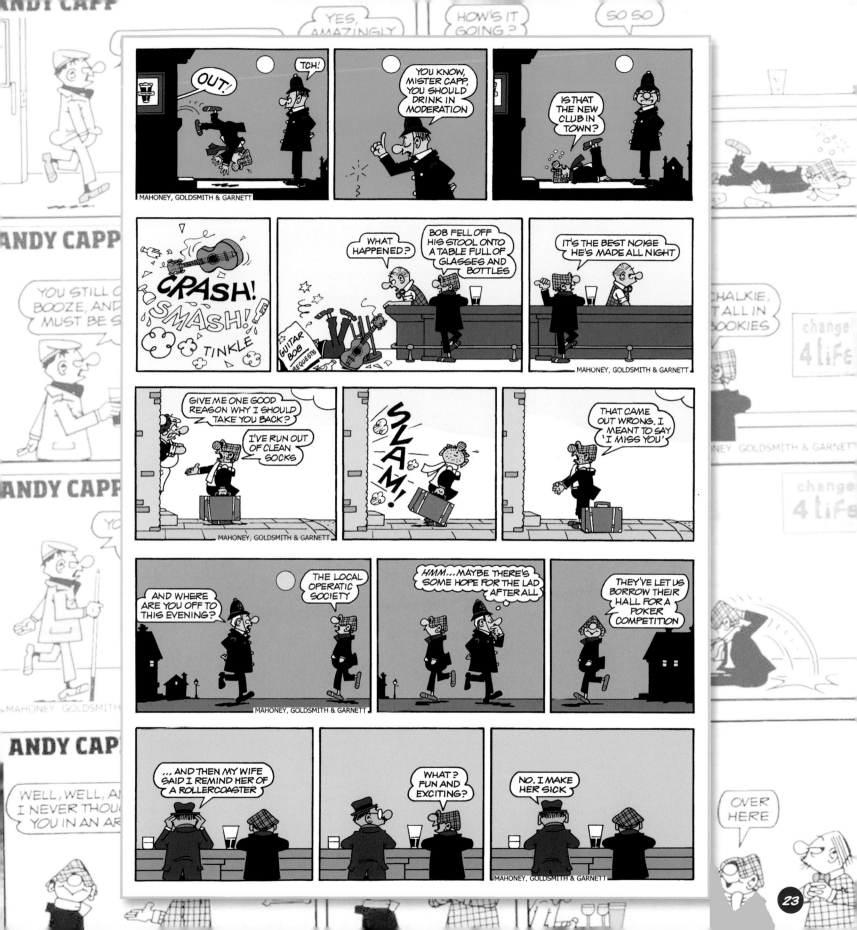

GUITAR BOB'S TOP ROMANTIC HITS

Hi guys and girls, peace to you all. It's that time of year where love fills the air – can't you just feel it all around, man? Now, there's nothing better than music to melt the hearts of someone you fancy. And there's no shortage of sweet and soppy songs to play, or even sing, to that lucky person you've plucked up the courage to ask out on a date. So, here's my guide to the best, or should I say cheesiest, love songs out there...

(1) YOU ARE THE SUNSHINE OF MY LIFE by Stevie Wonder

With lines like: "I feel this is the beginning, Though I've loved you for a million years, And if I thought our love was ending, I'd find myself drowning in my own tears…" how could you possibly not have a girl drooling over the red rose you've just had delivered to your table?

YUK, A GIRL DROOLING OVER THE TABLE – THAT'S ENOUGH TO MAKE ME GAG ON MY BEER. JACK WON'T LIKE THAT.

(2) WONDERFUL WORLD by Sam Cooke

Who could fail to swoon at the lyrics: "But I do know that I love you, And I know that if you loved me too, What a wonderful world this would be?" Old Sam clearly knew the way to a lass's heart. Just grab your date by the arm, croon those words and she'll be like putty in your hands.

ANDY SANG THAT SONG TO ME WHEN WE WERE FIRST DATING, IT TURNS OUT HE WAS ACTUALLY SINGING IT TO MY PURSE.

(3) (EVERYTHING I DO) I DO IT FOR YOU by Bryan Adams

Ladies, ladies, are you ready for this one? Once a date warbles the words: "Look into my eyes, you will see, What you mean to me, Search your heart, search your soul, And when you find me there, you'll search no more…" you'll be blown away. Of course you girls could sing the lines to a fella and I'm sure he'll go weak at the knees.

ONLY BECAUSE HE'S PROBABLY HAD SIX PINTS OF JACK'S STRONG ALES TO DROWN OUT THE SOUND OF ALL THAT SOPPY NOISE.

(4) THE POWER OF LOVE by Jennifer Rush

I'll just go straight into this as these words need no explaining: "'Cause I am your lady, And you are my man, Whenever you reach for me, I'll do all that I can…" Tell me that hasn't made you feel like flopping into the arms of someone you fancy.

ALRIGHT THEN, THAT HASN'T MADE ME FEEL LIKE FLOPPING INTO THE ARMS OF SOMEONE I FANCY. BUT IT HAS MADE ME FEEL LIKE ASKING JACK FOR A SICK BUCKET.

(5) LAY BACK IN THE ARMS OF SOMEONE by Smokie

Churn out these words to your hot date: "So baby just call on me, When you want all of me, I'll be your lover, I'll be your friend…" and believe me you will have them so entranced you'll never need to say anything else all night. And if you can do it in that gravelly, sexy voice the lead singer of Smokie used to have, you'll probably have the rest of the women in whatever room you're in melting, too.

ANDY TRIED THAT TO SOME LASS ONCE BUT SHE JUST THOUGHT HE HAD A SORE THROAT AND LAUGHED AT HIM – ALL NIGHT.

(6) CAN'T HELP FALLING IN LOVE by Elvis Presley

Who can forget these lines: "Take my hand, take my whole life through, For I can't help falling in love with you?" Alright, I doubt anyone could sing it quite like Elvis, but just lower your voice a bit, raise one eyebrow and curl your top lip and, voila, you'll look like a proper smoothie and your lucky lass will feel like the only girl in the world.

YOU'LL LOOK LIKE A PROPER SOMETHING, AND I'M TOO POLITE TO SAY WHAT IT IS.

(7) I WANT TO KNOW WHAT LOVE IS by Foreigner

Well, what can I say? Just look at these lines: "I wanna know what love is, I want you to show me, I wanna know what love is, I know you can show me…" Oh my gosh, I'm getting emotional just writing them down. If you can't get to a girl's heart with this corker, you may as well give up now.

OH DEAR, IF SOMEONE SANG THAT TO ME THE ONLY THING I'D SHOW THEM IS THE DOOR OUT.

(8) LOVE ME DO by The Beatles

John, Paul, George and Ringo certainly knew a thing or two about lovey dovey lyrics. I mean, they sang "Love, love me do, I know I love you, I'll always be true, So please, love me do…" You can't get more straightforward than that and if you want to go directly to your date's heart, just belt this out.

I SAW A LAD TRY THIS LAST YEAR ON VALENTINE'S DAY AND THE LASS JUST TOLD ME TO STOP SERVING HIM COS SHE THOUGHT HE WAS SOZZLED.

(9) HOW DEEP IS YOUR LOVE by the Bee Gees

They may have had very high-pitched voices, but the Bee Gee boys were top of the pops when it came to soppy songs. I mean listen to this: "I believe in you, You know the door to my very soul, You're the light in my deepest darkest hour…" I'm choking up just repeating those words. Take it from me, you'll be well in if you play, or sing, this song to a girl this Valentine's night.

IF I HEAR THIS SONG ON THE JUKE BOX TONIGHT, I'LL CHOKE WHOEVER PUT IT ON.

(10) I WANNA MARRY YOU by Bruce Springsteen

He's not called The Boss for nothing and The Boss was clearly in charge when it comes to writing this love song. How about these lyrics for telling it how it is: "Little girl I wanna marry you, Oh yeah, little girl I wanna marry you, Yes I do, Little girl I wanna marry you…" If that doesn't get the message across, what will?

HE MIGHT BE THE BOSS NOW, BUT AS SOON AS THAT LITTLE GIRL SAYS "YES" HE CAN KISS GOODBYE TO THAT TITLE.

ANDY'S GUIDE TO VALENTINES

As you no doubt know, I've been a bit of a hit with the lasses over the years. My magnetic charm and razor-sharp wit can mesmerise them and, before they know it, they're lining up drinks for me. But I've noticed some fellas don't share my gift and often turn into gibbering wrecks in the company of women. Why not follow my advice on how to melt the hearts of lasses everywhere...

CHAT-UP LINES
Try not to make them too cheesy. Saying guff like: "Heaven must be missing an angel," to a lass could make her choke on her half a lager and lime. Be more subtle.

> LIKE THE NIGHT HE BELLOWED AT ONE GIRL: "HELLO, LUV, GET 'EM IN AND THEN YOU CAN TAKE ME TO THE DOGS." VERY SUBTLE.

> I MUST BE LISTENING TO THE WRONG ANDY, I'VE NEVER KNOWN HIM TO BUY DRINKS OR FISH AND CHIPS FOR ANY GIRL, EVER.

SHARE COSTS
In this day and age of equality, fellas aren't expected to buy all the drinks and fish and chips on the way home. Which is a bit of a relief to me, to be honest.

FIB ABOUT YOUR AGE
Never appear knowledgeable about anything that happened more than 20 years ago. In my case I can't remember what happened yesterday let alone two decades ago so I'm OK.

HUMOUR
Lasses love it if you make them laugh. And when I'm around they often end up in stitches. You know you're on to a winner if a girl is weeping tears of joy.

PLAY IT COOL
When you first clap eyes on a lovely lass on her own at the bar, don't go steaming in with chat-up lines and stuff. That'll only scare 'em off. Start by pretending you haven't noticed 'em and then slip over quietly. You'll get much more respect.

BE YOURSELF
There's nowt a lass likes less than fellas pretending to be something they're not. Be straight with 'em from the word go, that way there are no 'orrible shocks for them further down the line.

SWEET NOTHINGS
Always tell a lass what she wants to hear. When a girl asks what you think of her new hairdo, or dress, or something, she does not want the truth, especially if she looks like she's been dragged through a hedge backwards.

> THIS FROM THE SAME BLOKE WHO TOLD ONE WOMAN SHE'D NEED A CHISEL TO REMOVE ALL THAT MAKE-UP.

MUSIC
I get Chalkie to put some soppy love song on the juke box when I see a lass I fancy, then stare over at her mouthing the words.

> OH, YEAH? I'VE YET TO HEAR HIM TELL ANY GIRL HE'S NOTHING BUT A LAZY, WORKSHY, SCROUNGING, DRUNKEN BUM.

> THE LAST TIME I DID THAT THE GIRL ASKED ME WHO THE BONKERS BLOKE TALKING TO HIMSELF AT THE BAR WAS.

25

CHALKIE'S CHUCKLES

"I hate to have to tell you this," said the doctor in a sad, compassionate voice. "But you have been diagnosed with a highly contagious disease. We will have to quarantine you and you'll only be fed cheese and ham."
"That's terrible!" said the distraught young man, quickly sitting down before he could faint. 'I don't know if I could handle being in quarantine…and the diet…what's with the cheese and ham anyway? I've never heard of such a diet before?!" "It's not exactly a diet," responded the doctor in a serious tone. "It's just the only food that will fit under the door!"

Man walks into a dentist.
Receptionist: "Can I help you?"
Man: "I keep thinking I'm a moth."
Receptionist: "This is a dentists, you need a psychiatrist."
Man: "Yes, I know."
Receptionist: "Well, why did you come in here?"
Man: "Because your light was on!"

"Tell me, Gary, how did you manage to get so very drunk last night?" asked the vicar.
"Well you see, Father, it was like this. I got into very bad company after winning a bottle of whiskey at a raffle."
"But you were with Nick, Dave, and Johnny and they don't drink."
"That's what I mean, Father…"

A man heard his wife in the kitchen say: "Chicken or chilli con carne?"
He shouted back: "Chicken, please."
His wife replied: "You're getting soup, fatty – I'm talking to the cat."

What did the tectonic plate say to the other tectonic plate when he bumped into him?
Sorry, my fault.

Two astronauts walk out of a bar on the moon. "What did you think of that place?" one of the astronauts asked.
"The drinks were OK," the second astronaut replied. "But there was no atmosphere."

A farmer's dog goes missing and he is inconsolable.
His wife says to him, "Why don't you put an ad in the paper to get him back?"
The farmer does this, but after two weeks and no phone calls, the dog is still missing.
"What did you write in the paper?" asked his wife.
"Here boy," said the farmer.

ASK ANDY

GOT A PROBLEM? CONSIDER IT SOLVED!

Dear Andy,
My wife says I love beer more than her. In fact, she says I should have married a pint glass as I spend so much time looking longingly at one. Trouble is, I think she's right.

How can I convince her she means more to me than the drink – when I don't really believe it myself?

Steve, Blackpool.

ANDY'S REPLY

Tricky one, that, Steve lad. Ye could try telling her that when yer staring longingly at your pint yer lost in a world of memories, recalling all the happy times you've had together as a couple, like, and looking forward to even more happy times ahead. But don't make the same mistake as me and let her catch you telling your pint, "I love you more than anything in the world". Flo has never really forgiven me.

Dear Andy,
I'm playing in my first football cup final next weekend and I'm so nervous I can barely sleep.

You're a seasoned player, what do you suggest I do to stay calm?

Ian, Lancaster.

ANDY'S REPLY

Well, Ian, son, my gaffer won't thank me for telling ye this, but just go down the pub every night for a drink with yer mates. It might not be healthy, but then getting no sleep can't be good for you either. And what would you rather do, turn up with a bit of a hangover or run the risk of nodding off just before the game starts?

I ignore the rule about not drinking before games (my gaffer has accused me of ignoring it right up until kick-off) and I feel raring to go once I stagger across that white line. Good luck, lad.

Dear Andy,
There's this girl I really fancy but I think she's a bit too classy for me. I don't want to make a prat of myself by saying the wrong sort of things to her when I chat her up cos I'm not the cleverest lad around. As a man who understands women, what would you do in my situation?

Brian, Norwich.

ANDY'S REPLY

You've picked the right man here, Brian. I'm known as something of an old romantic round my town, although some lasses seem too keen on emphasising the "old" bit.

She sounds like a bit of a posh lass, this one. What you need to do is read the culture section of a broadsheet the night before you plan on making a move, then dazzle her with yer knowledge of current affairs and stuff. She'll be like putty in yer hands.

But be careful with some of that clever stuff – one plummy lass I was once chatting up asked me what I thought of Canaletto and she nearly choked on her pina colada through laughter when I told her I didn't like any spaghetti dishes.

29

LOOK BACK WITH ANDY

Everybody usually remembers where they were when major events occurred but, for some reason, Andy's memory is a bit hazy!! So, to remind him, here are a few classic Andy strips from some famous dates in history...

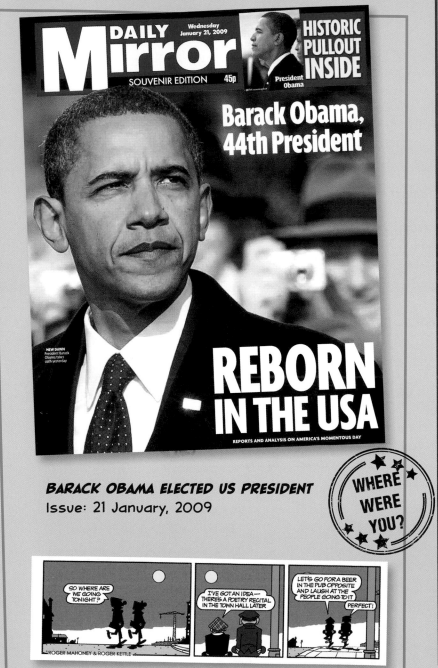

BARACK OBAMA ELECTED US PRESIDENT
Issue: 21 January, 2009

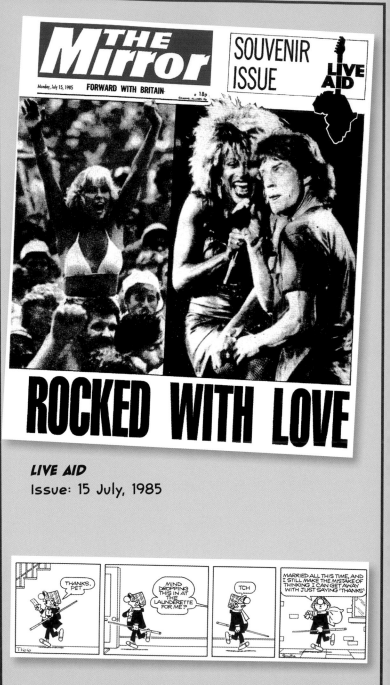

LIVE AID
Issue: 15 July, 1985

JACK'S PUB QUIZ

TELEVISION

1. Which comedians dressed as night club bouncers and called themselves 'The Management'?

2. June Brown plays which character in EastEnders?

3. "I don't believe it" was a catchphrase of which TV grump?

4. Terry Wogan, Les Dawson and Lily Savage have all hosted which gameshow?

5. Which Australian series is set in fictional Summer Bay?

6. Fox Mulder and Dana Scully were the main characters in which television series?

7. Which actress played the Vicar of Dibley?

8. Of which television series was Jack Bauer the protagonist?

9. What is the name of the theme tune from the US sitcom, Friends ?

10. Who is the regular host of BBC's Match of the Day on Saturday night?

11. In which year was the soap EastEnders first broadcast?

12. Which BBC medical drama was a spin-off from Casualty?

MARCH

SUNDAY

1

MONDAY

2

TUESDAY

3

WEDNESDAY

4

THURSDAY

5

FRIDAY

6

SATURDAY

7

SUNDAY

8

MONDAY

9

TUESDAY

10

WEDNESDAY

11

THURSDAY

12

FRIDAY

13

SATURDAY

14

SUNDAY

15

MONDAY

16

THINGS
TO DO

TUESDAY

17

St Patrick's Day (Northern Ireland)

WEDNESDAY

18

THURSDAY

19

FRIDAY

20

SATURDAY

21

SUNDAY

22

MONDAY

23

TUESDAY

24

WEDNESDAY

25

THURSDAY

26

FRIDAY

27

SATURDAY

28

SUNDAY

29

MONDAY

30

TUESDAY

31

SPORTING EVENTS TO KEEP AN EYE OUT FOR
Football – Capital One Cup Final – 1st March
Horse Racing – Cheltenham Festival – 10th March to 13th March
Formula One – Australian Grand Prix – 12th March to 15th March

THINGS TO DO

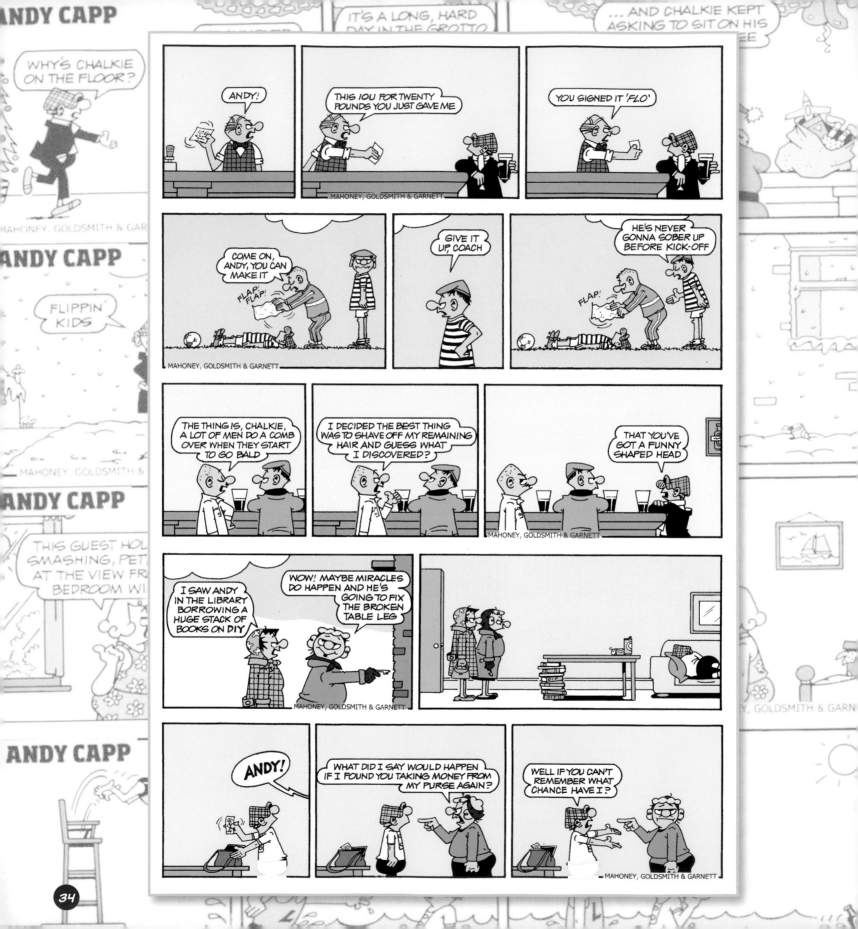

FLO'S KITCHEN

Hello folks, and welcome to the first of my cookery pages.

I'll tell you how to prepare great dishes from around the world, starting with everyone's favourite Italian dish – Spaghetti Bolognese.

This is an easy-to-make meal and, topped off with parmesan cheese, makes a tasty treat.

INGREDIENTS

Right, lads and lasses, for this dish you will need:

500g Fresh Beef Mince
400g Dried Spaghetti
2 Tins of Plum/Chopped Tomatoes
2 Medium Onions, peeled and finely diced
2 Carrots, trimmed and finely diced
2 Cloves of Garlic, peeled and finely diced
75g Freshly grated Parmesan Cheese, plus extra for grating
2 tbsp Tomato Puree
1 Beef Stock Cube
Salt
Mixed herbs
Olive oil
Got that lot sorted? Great, now let's get down to the actual cooking...

THE PARMESAN COMES IN HANDY FOLKS, I USE LOTS OF IT TO DISGUISE FLO'S BURNT BOLOGNESE, HEH HEH.

METHOD

Place a heavy saucepan onto a medium heat hob. Add olive oil and gently fry your onions, garlic and carrots. Increase the heat slightly, add the mince and stir until the meat is browned all over.

Stir in your tomatoes. Add your herbs, tomato puree and stock cube.

Stir with a wooden spoon and bring to a simmer. Reduce the heat to low-medium, put the lid on and leave to simmer for about an hour and 15 minutes. Stir occasionally.

And if you go gossiping over the fence with your neighbour, like Flo does, don't forget about the flipping thing bubbling away on the cooker. She burnt it to a flaming' crisp last time.

Tch, don't listen to him. Just as the sauce is nearly ready, add the parmesan to taste. Put another pan of water on to boil and add salt and the spaghetti. Cook to whatever it says on the packet – cos I can never remember how long to do it...

That would account for all the black spaghetti I've seen in our bin when I'm throwing my empties away.

Oh shush, Andy. Anyway, once the spaghetti is ready, drain it and add it to the pan with the sauce. Give it a stir. Serve with grated parmesan.

HOPE YOU ALL LOVE IT.

ALL YOU'LL NEED NOW IS A HAMMER AND CHISEL TO BREAK UP FLO'S SPAGHETTI, HA HA. ONLY JOKING, PET, HONEST.

The vicar, along with Flo, is always having a go at me about spending my hard-borrowed cash on the nags. But they don't understand the delight of picking a winner and getting one over on the bookies.

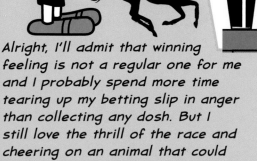

Alright, I'll admit that winning feeling is not a regular one for me and I probably spend more time tearing up my betting slip in anger than collecting any dosh. But I still love the thrill of the race and cheering on an animal that could provide me with beer money for the night. Here are my top tips...

BE CAREFUL

If some bloke down the pub tells you there's a dead cert running at whatever race that day, don't back it. He's probably got the tip from some other flippin' bloke down a pub who knows nowt.

> HE'S SPEAKING FROM BITTER EXPERIENCE.

RESEARCH

Folk will tell you to study the form of a horse, or rider, and they're right. I spend ages scouring the racing pages in Jack's paper to find out how well some nag or other has been doing recently before slapping Flo's cash on it.

> AND IT REALLY CHEESES HIM OFF WHEN I GET TO HAVE A GO AND PICK A HORSE BECAUSE I LIKE THE JOCKEY'S COLOURS – ESPECIALLY WHEN IT WINS AND THE ONES HE'S BEEN STUDYING DON'T.

> HE SPENDS MOST OF HIS TIME STARING AT THE BACK OF THE PACK WONDERING WHERE THE HELL HIS HORSE IS... AGAIN.

KEEP QUIET

Never brag about winning, there's always some flaming fella in earshot who you probably owe money to. Before you know it, that wad of cash you have in your hand will have vanished.

> IN HIS CASE, IT'S EVERY BLOKE WITHIN EARSHOT WHO HE'LL OWE MONEY.

JOCKEYS

Take a close look at the riders. If you spot any with black eyes, bruised faces or other such injuries then DON'T flippin' back them. It's a sure sign they spend most of their time falling off.

> YEA, BUT ANDY ONCE BACKED A HORSE WITH SUCH A JOCKEY WHO HAD FALLEN OFF THREE TIMES IN ONE MEETING – BELIEVING NO JOCKEY COULD FALL OFF FOUR TIMES. HE DID.

BARS

Racing and drinking go hand in hand, but if your luck is down when it comes to the horses then try propping up the bar. The best time to go is when the races are on as everyone is out watching it, so you'll have the place to yourself. Try starting a tab with the bar tender, then sneak out when the crowds come back in.

EXCITEMENT

Get as near to the winning post as possible cos you can't beat the thrill of seeing those nags thundering towards the finish knowing one of them could make you richer than you were when the race started.

CHALKIE'S CHUCKLES

A duck walks into a bar and asks: "Got any bread?"

Barman: "Err... No."

Duck: "Got any bread?"

Barman: "No – this is a pub – we sell beer, not bread."

Duck: "Got any bread?"

Barman: "No, we have no bread."

Duck: "Got any bread?"

Barman: "No, we haven't got any flippin' bread. This is a pub, not a bakehouse!"

Duck: "Got any bread?"

Barman: "Are you flippin' deaf or daft? We haven't got any flippin' bread, ask me again and I'll nail your flippin' bill to the bar!"

(Pause)

Duck: "Got any nails?"

Barman: "No"

(Pause)

Duck: "Got any bread?"

Three construction workers are discussing their lunchbox contents. Englishman: "If I get the same old jam butty tomorrow I will jump off this damn building." The Irish lad says the same thing and the French man also says he'll jump if he gets bread and cheese again.

Next day's lunch break, the Englishman has a different butty in his lunchbox, the Irishman also has a change but the French man has the same old, so curses and jumps off the building.

At the funeral his wife is heard telling the other lads: "I just don't understand it, he always made his own lunch."

Teacher: "Jimmy, if you had five biscuits and I asked for one, how many would you have?"

Jimmy: "Five."

Why does history keep repeating itself? Because we weren't listening the first time!

What do you call a chicken in a shell-suit? An egg.

Knock Knock, Who's There? Someone who can't reach the doorbell!

Why did the nurse tip toe past the medicine cabinet? Because she didn't want to wake the sleeping pills.

ANDY CAPP'S WORST KITS..........

As regular followers of my adventures will already know, I'm famed for my sartorial elegance and flair. Flat cap, single breasted jacket, scarf – it's a classic combination.

OK, sartorial flair might be pushing it a bit but few can deny that I basically nailed it in the fashion stakes many years ago and as they say – if it ain't broke, why fix it?

Sadly the same can't be said for some of our more famous football teams. I suppose it can't be easy designing a new kit in the same colours year after year and you know what it's like with these creative design types – they're always looking to do something a bit different. Unfortunately though, different isn't always better – as these horrors will testify...

PETER SCHMEICHEL – MANCHESTER UNITED

Schmeichel famously designed one of his own kits and, on this evidence, it is easy to see why he didn't become the next Fred Perry after retiring from the game.

We'll give him the benefit of the doubt and assume that this green, red and blue slashed horror was actually designed to put off opposing strikers. Either way, I'd hate to see how he decorates his house...

SUNDERLAND – 1992 FA CUP FINAL KIT

There's a lot to like about Sunderland. Great team, great fans and they're also from the North East of England, just like yours truly. Plus at this point they were sponsored by the Vaux brewery in Sunderland – one of my favourite old breweries.

Sadly this square polka dot number worn to the 1992 FA Cup Final isn't one of those things. I mean, square polka dots? What were they thinking? Sunderland lost that cup final and a few year's later Vaux sadly became defunct. I'm not saying these things are connected, but...

NORWICH CITY

Green and yellow. Always a tricky combination to pull off, unless you happen to be Brazilian. Now don't be offended Norwich fans, but I'm going to suggest the designer was working with one hand tied behind their backs from the outset, but that doesn't excuse this monstrosity in 1992. I have no idea what the pattern is and, as it hurts my eyes to keep staring at it, I'm just going to stop...

DAVID SEAMAN - ENGLAND, EURO '96

Three Lions, a nation united behind their team, that demolition of Holland, Gazza's goal against Scotland and Pearce's spot-kick redemption. So many happy memories from the summer of 1996 and then I get reminded of this jersey! What is it about goalkeepers? I guess you have to be a bit tapped to play between the sticks, the footballing equivalent of the rock band drummer – but even so, have some self respect!

LIVERPOOL AWAY KIT

Mistakes happen, and there's nowt wrong with that providing you learn from them. For example, sometimes I forget to take my wallet to the pub with me but happily the lads have learnt to buy my beer, so it's all good.

WHAT WALLET?

However, someone clearly hasn't been paying attention to the mistakes of past football kits – otherwise they would never have conceived this effort. What's it supposed to mean? What are all those red and black flecks – they remind me of those horrible flecked trousers that were popular for a week back in 1986.

Why, why, why?

LOOK BACK WITH ANDY

EEverybody usually remembers where they were when major events occurred but, for some reason, Andy's memory is a bit hazy!! So, to remind him, here are a few classic Andy strips from some famous dates in history...

QUEEN ELIZABETH II DIAMOND JUBILEE
Issue: 4 June, 2012

THE KRAYS SENT TO PRISON
Issue: 6 March, 1969

TARGET WORDS PUZZLE

Using the letters in the grid only once, make as many words as possible of four or more letters, excluding proper names and plurals. Every word must contain the central, shaded letter. You can make at least one word containing all nine letters.

T	E	S
L	I	A
L	E	G

1 LETTER

HOW WELL DID YOU DO?
23 excellent
20 good
16 average

Using the letters in the grid only once, make as many words as possible of four or more letters, excluding proper names and plurals. Every word must contain the two shaded letters. You can make at least one word containing all nine letters.

C	E	H
T	A	R
S	D	C

2 LETTER

HOW WELL DID YOU DO?
15 excellent
13 good
10 average

APRIL

WEDNESDAY

1

THURSDAY

2

FRIDAY

3

Good Friday

SATURDAY

4

SUNDAY

5

Easter Sunday

MONDAY

6

Easter Monday

TUESDAY

7

WEDNESDAY

8

THURSDAY

9

FRIDAY

10

SATURDAY

11

SUNDAY

12

MONDAY

13

TUESDAY

14

WEDNESDAY

15

THURSDAY

16

THINGS TO DO

FRIDAY

17

SATURDAY

18

SUNDAY

19

MONDAY

20

TUESDAY

21

WEDNESDAY

22

THURSDAY

23

FRIDAY

24

SATURDAY

25

SUNDAY

26

MONDAY

27

TUESDAY

28

WEDNESDAY

29

THURSDAY

30

THINGS TO DO

SPORTING EVENTS TO KEEP AN EYE OUT FOR
Horse Racing – 2015 Crabbie's Grand National Festival – 9th April to 11th April
Golf – US Masters – 9th April to 12th April
Snooker – World Snooker Championships – 18th April to 4th May
Athletics – London Marathon – 26th April

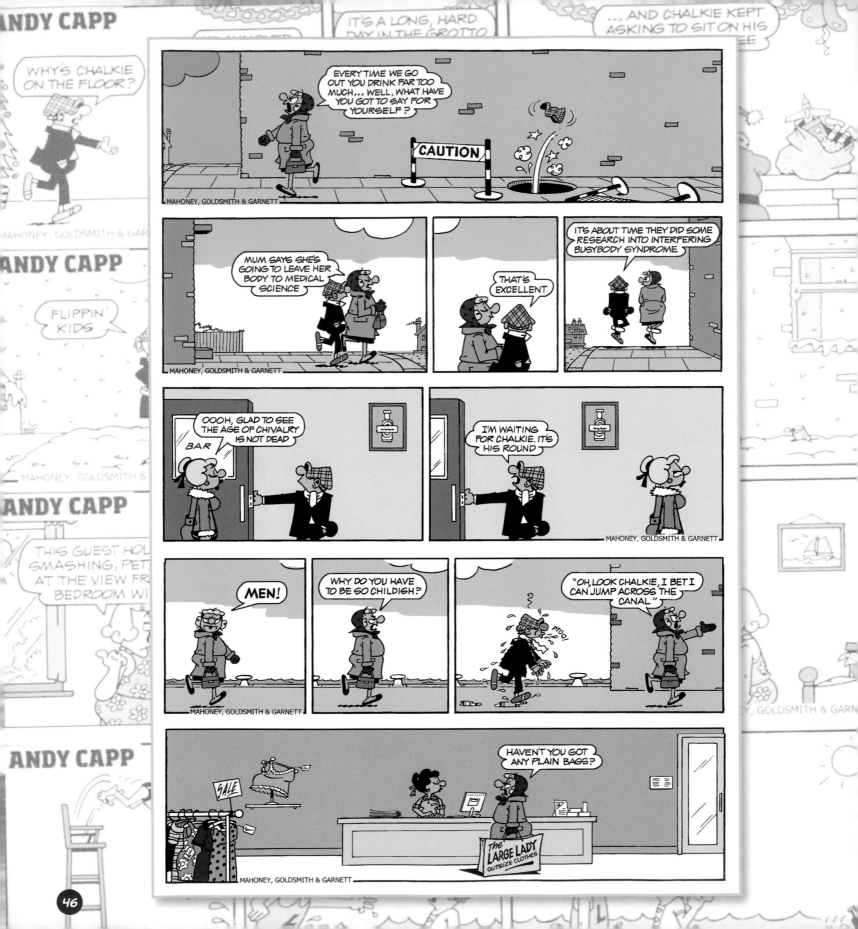

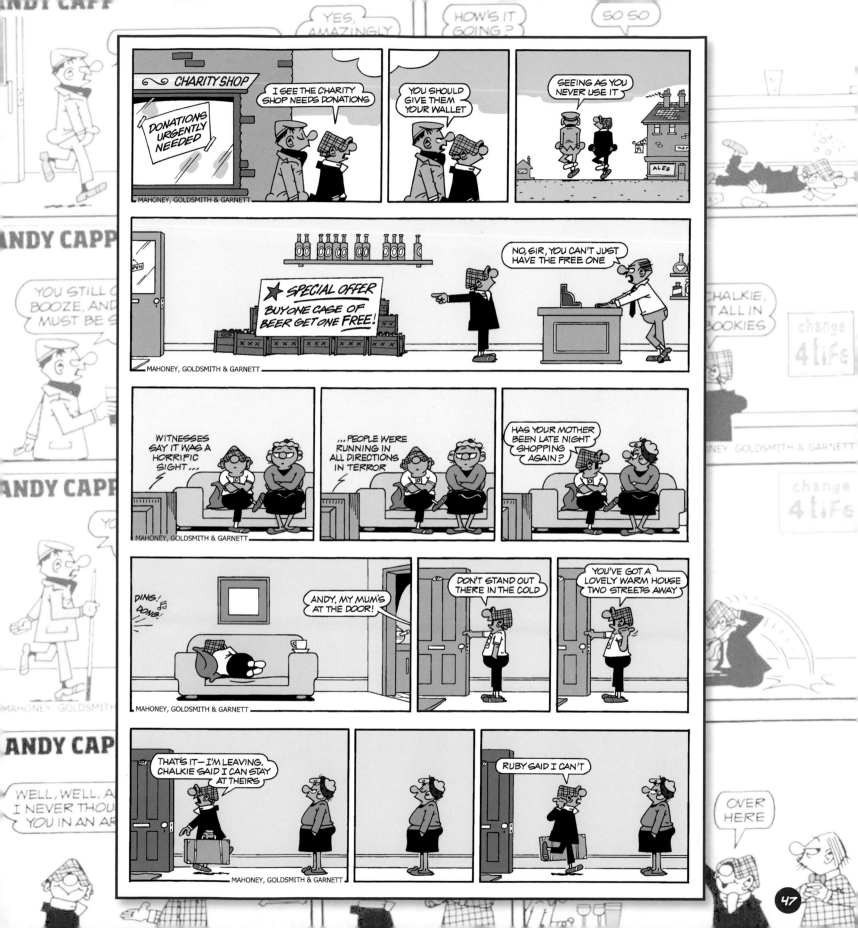

THE VICAR'S EASTER SERMON

Of course, we all know Jesus was crucified, rose from the dead and ascended to Heaven to take away our sins - the ultimate sacrifice for the greater good of a mankind that was teetering perilously close to the abyss.

And talking of teetering perilously close to the edge, I would just like to remind certain male members of my congregation who are fond of a drink or two that the church is not a place to come and dry out after falling in the canal. Mrs Bryant, the cleaner, was most upset at the amount of brown dirty water pooling on the pew at the back last Saturday morning.

Anyway, back to Easter. Of course, there were people who did not believe Jesus had risen. It was a trick, they said at first. But once they realised the truth, they stopped their sneering and rejoiced.

And that's what I want us all to do this weekend, rejoice and celebrate. Although I would rather not have a repeat of last year's Easter party in the church hall where one of my flock, who shall remain nameless (although we can probably all guess who he is) downed the rum punch in one, straight from the bowl as others were waiting patiently in the queue for a cup. He then fell backwards and knocked Mrs Pilkington's new fruit bowl-style hat clean off. We didn't know afterwards which bits of fruit were from the hat or the rum punch.

So, go out there my children and celebrate the resurrection. And remember not to get drunk on wine (or whatever that brown, murky stuff Andy Capp and his pals drink in the pub is) but be filled with the spirit of the Lord.

HELLO TO MY CHERISHED FLOCK OUT THERE AND MAY I WISH YOU ALL A HAPPY EASTER.

CAN I ALSO TAKE THIS OPPORTUNITY TO REFLECT ON THE MEANING OF THIS IMPORTANT PERIOD IN THE RELIGIOUS CALENDAR...

ANDY'S GUIDE TO SPRING

Well, spring has finally sprung. I love this time of year. It rains less, the nights are starting to get longer and not as grey and people seem to be happier (except Flo's mum when she meets me). So, put away yer winter clothes, and let me guide you through making the most out of this season of change...

EASTER Two days off in one weekend, how about that? It means there'll be more people in the pubs during the day which, apart from being right sociable, means there'll be more people to buy me drinks when I'm skint.

> WHEN HE'S SKINT? WHEN IS HE EVER NOT? THE ONLY TIME HE'S GOT MONEY IS WHEN FLO'S WITH HIM AND HE GOES TO THE BAR WITH HER PURSE.

STROLL Make the most of the lighter nights by having a walk. I see plenty of people passing our window doing just that. Most of them are mates of mine who are heading down the pub so being a sociable sort, I always flippin' well join 'em.

> AND HE CATCHES THEM UP PRETTY QUICKLY OWING TO THE FACT HE HAS NO CASH IN HIS POCKETS WEIGHING HIM DOWN.

> I MAY AS WELL GO AND LIVE SOMEWHERE ELSE FOR A FEW DAYS. NO ROOM ON THE SOFA, NO CHANCE OF WATCHING MY SOAPS AND FALLING OVER EMPTIES WHILE A BUNCH OF DRUNKS YELL AT THE TELLY IS NOT MY IDEA OF FUN.

FOOTBALL With the season finish fast approaching and teams chasing championships and promotion while others fight to avoid relegation, there's practically blanket coverage on the telly. So get yersels a case of ale and settle down in front of the box with a few pals for a feast of footie.

APRIL SHOWERS Alright, there is one draw back to spring – but look on the bright side, the pubs are open. This is a great opportunity to socialise with pals and have lots of drinks bought for you.

> AS IF IT MAKES A BLIND BIT OF DIFFERENCE WHAT THE WEATHER IS DOING. HE'LL BE IN THAT FLAMIN' PUB COME RAIN OR SHINE.

PICNICS There's nowt better than grabbing a crate of ale and heading off with yer fishing rod for a nice quiet day by the river bank. If you're lucky, the missus will bring another crate down later when you've run out and help cart your gear home, too.

> FLO ONLY ACTUALLY GETS ROUND TO THE GARDENING ONCE SHE'S CLEARED UP ALL THE EMPTIES ANDY HAS BEEN CHUCKING OUT OF THE WINDOW OVER WINTER WHEN THE BIN'S FULL.

PLANTING THINGS This is the time to get out in the garden and grow stuff. I've watched Flo do it and it looks like she's really enjoying it. She clearly finds it therapeutic after a morning's cleaning and washing up and the garden's looking lovely. Mind you, I need to get her to rein it in a bit – my pigeon shed is filling up with all her tools.

49

CHALKIE'S CHUCKLES

Bill walks into a post office one day to see a middle-aged man standing at the counter enthusiastically writing addresses on bright pink envelopes covered with hearts. He then takes out a scent bottle and starts spraying perfume over them. Bill's curiosity gets the better of him and he walks over to the man and asks him what he's doing.
"I'm sending out 1,000 Valentine's Day cards signed, 'Guess who?'" says the man.
"Why on earth are you doing that?" asks Bill.
"Because I'm a divorce lawyer," replies the man.

So I rang up a local building firm, and said: "I want a skip outside my house."
He replied: "I'm not stopping you."

Man walks into a bar, and orders three drams of whisky, four pints of Guinness and eight shots of Jagermeister.
As soon as the barman pours each drink, the man immediately downs it.
The barman looks up, "Are you alright there, Sir? You're drinking them pretty quickly!" The man looks over at his third pint of Guinness and says, 'Well, you've got to drink quickly when you've got what I have."
The barman stops pouring the fourth pint, and asks, "Why? What have you got then?"
The man looks up, sighs, and says, "About one pound fifty."

A man goes to the vet about his dog's fleas. The vet says: "I'm sorry, I'll have to put this dog down." The man is incredulous and asks why. The vet says: "Because he's far too heavy."

Mary was asleep in bed when her husband, Patrick, crashed through the front door at 3am waking her up. He staggered through the hallway and tried to get up the stairs.
"What are you doing?" Mary shouted.
Patrick replied, "I'm trying to get this gallon of beer up the stairs."
"Leave it down there, Patrick!" Mary bellowed. "I can't," Patrick replied. "I've drunk it."

A man walks into a bar, sits down, and orders a drink. "Hey, nice tie!" comes out of nowhere. He looks up at the barman to see if he had said anything, but since he was on the other side of the bar the man just ignores it.
"Hey! Nice shirt!" The man looks up but, again, the barman is engaged elsewhere. "Hey! Nice suit!" The man then calls the barman over and asks him why he keeps talking to him.
"It's not me, it's the complimentary peanuts," says the barman.

Two guys are walking down the street when a mugger jumps out at them, waving a knife around and demanding all their money. They both get their wallets out, and one guy hands his friend a £20 note saying: "Here's that money I owe you."

LOOK BACK WITH ANDY

Everybody usually remembers where they were when major events occurred but, for some reason, Andy's memory is a bit hazy!! So, to remind him, here are a few classic Andy strips from some famous dates in history...

US PRESIDENT RICHARD NIXON RESIGNS
Issue: 10 August, 1974

BEATLES ARRIVE IN NEW YORK, USA
Issue: 8 February, 1964

WHERE WERE YOU?

JACK'S PUB QUIZ

HISTORY

1. President John F. Kennedy was assassinated in which city in 1963?

2. Who led the Free French forces during World War II?

3. Which town was destroyed in AD79 when Mount Vesuvius erupted?

4. Which Soviet cosmonaut was the first man in space?

5. In which European city would you see the ruins of the Colosseum?

6. The 'unsinkable' liner, RMS Titanic, sank on her maiden voyage in what year?

7. Who was the US President forced to resign over the Watergate scandal?

8. Which Russian Tsar abdicated in 1917?

9. Golda Meir became the first female Prime Minister of which country in 1969?

10. In which year was the Battle of the Somme fought during World War I?

11. Which English king was known as 'The Lionheart'?

12. In which year did Guy Fawkes and others devise their unsuccessful 'Gunpowder Plot'?

FRIDAY

1

SATURDAY

2

SUNDAY

3

MONDAY

4

Early May bank holiday

TUESDAY

5

WEDNESDAY

6

THURSDAY

7

FRIDAY

8

SATURDAY

9

SUNDAY

10

MONDAY

11

TUESDAY

12

WEDNESDAY

13

THURSDAY

14

FRIDAY

15

SATURDAY

16

THINGS TO DO

SUNDAY

17

MONDAY

18

TUESDAY

19

WEDNESDAY

20

THURSDAY

21

FRIDAY

22

SATURDAY

23

SUNDAY

24

MONDAY

25

Spring bank holiday

TUESDAY

26

WEDNESDAY

27

THURSDAY

28

FRIDAY

29

SATURDAY

30

SUNDAY

31

THINGS TO DO

SPORTING EVENTS TO KEEP AN EYE OUT FOR
Golf – BMW PGA Championship – 19th May to 24th May
Cricket – England v New Zealand 1st Test – 21st May to 25th May
Tennis – French Open – 25th May to 7th June
Cricket – England v New Zealand 2nd Test – 29th May to 2nd June
Football – FA Cup Final – 30th May

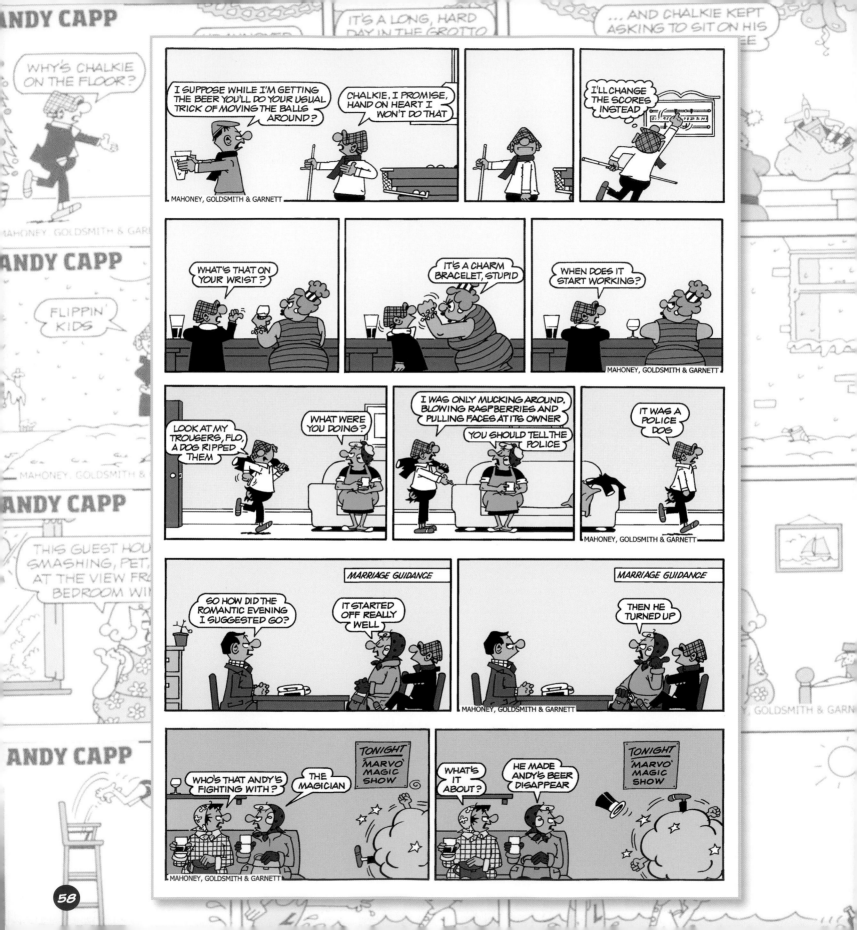

ANDY'S PIGEON PHILL

IT MIGHT BE MAY, BUT IT'S STILL COLD AT NIGHT SO ANDY HAS BROUGHT HIS BIRDS IN TO KEEP WARM. SADLY, THOUGH, FLO HAS BECOME DECIDEDLY FROSTY.

CAN YOU SPOT 10 DIFFERENCES BETWEEN THE PICTURES WHILE SHE THAWS OUT?

ANDY'S GUIDE TO POLITICS

Politicians – you don't see one for ages, then three come along at once. It must be polling time.

I've no doubt most of you are as dismissive of these people as I am, given that they only knock on your door when they want your flamin' vote and are never to be seen again. So here are a few thoughts on how to deal with them and how to spot when they're talking nonsense (which is most of the time)...

ARGUMENTS There's always someone in the pub who bangs on about flippin' politics and all it ever does is cause a row. I just tend to agree with everyone's views rather than argue – especially if they're buying me a drink while blethering away.

> I'VE NEVER SEEN ANYONE NOD SO MUCH ABOUT THINGS THEY DISAGREE WITH, JUST SO THEY CAN GET ANOTHER PINT OUT OF PEOPLE.

> THEY'D PROBABLY BE WISER CROSSING THE ROAD THEMSELVES IF HE'S HAD A FEW DRINKS AND IN A BELLIGERENT MOOD.

CAMPAIGNING When I was a nipper I always wondered why local councillors wore those daft rosettes that made them look like football fans in suits. Now I'm glad they do, it means I can spot them a mile off and cross the road to avoid them bloomin' well buttonholing me with their hot air.

GETTING REWARDS

Politicians will do anything to get you on their side, so ask them for a few favours. I usually manage to get a crate of ale from 'em or a week's worth of pigeon feed. Some folk might call this a bribe, I call it back scratching.

> EXCEPT THE ONLY BACK THAT'S BEING SCRATCHED IS HIS. HE NEVER VOTES ANYWAY, IT INTERFERES WITH HIS DRINKING AND LYING DOWN.

FIBS Local councillors promising the earth are being liberal with the flamin' truth. If they tell you your Council Tax will come down under their rule, expect it to flippin' well go up as soon as they get power (it really annoys Flo as she pays it). Likewise, if they pledge to do everything they can to keep open pubs threatened with closure, start looking for another boozer.

> IF ANDY WAS A COUNCILLOR HIS SOLE POLICY WOULD BE TO KEEP PUBS OPEN – ALL NIGHT, PROBABLY.

> NOT AT ALL LIKE A CERTAIN PERSON PROMISING FLO HE'LL ONLY BE GONE FOR AN HOUR OR SO THEN ONCE HE'S GOT HER CASH HE'S HERE FOR THE NIGHT THEN COMES UP WITH A MILLION AND ONE EXCUSES AS TO HOW THAT HAPPENED.

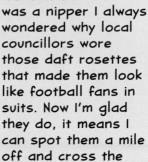

ALLEGIANCES It's best not to have any, as all parties will only let you down. Politics would be much better if it wasn't full of bloomin' politicians.

THE REAL WORLD It's astonishing how these people can promise to do all sorts of things such as keep hospitals, schools, community centres etc. open before they get your vote – then tell you, after they're in office, that those things are shutting down and that everything that led to it was beyond their control.

CHALKIE'S CHUCKLES

There's this bus full of ugly people, and it crashes and they all die.

When they get to Heaven, St Peter says: "I know it's a bit unfair all of you dying like that, so me and the big fella have decided to give you all one wish each before you come through the pearly gates."

So they form an orderly queue, and St Peter starts granting wishes.

"What's your wish?" he says to the lady at the front of the queue.

"I want to be beautiful, it's all I ever wanted," she replies. St Peter makes her stunning, proper drop dead gorgeous.

"What's your wish?" he asks the fella behind her.

"I'd like to be beautiful, too." he replies, so Peter makes him beautiful as well.

St Peter then gets a glance at the back of the queue, and at the very end there is a guy killing himself laughing. He ignores it and carries on.

"What's your wish?" he asks number three in line.

"Make me beautiful." And so he does.

This continues all the way down the queue: "I want to be beautiful" and "Make me beautiful" everyone asks, until he reaches the guy at the end.

"What's your wish?" he asks the last man.

Between fits of laughter, he replies "Make 'em all ugly again."

Three gents were drinking apple martinis in a bar and had got to the stage of arguing about details.
"I tell you it's spelled W-O-O-M," the first said loudly.
"No no, no," the second protested. "It's W-O-O-O-M."
"You're both wrong," the third ventured.
"I say it's W-O-O-M-B."
A passing gynaecologst spoke up. "You're getting close," she told them. "Actually, it's W-O-M-B."
They stared at her a moment, then stared at each other. Finally, one spoke:
"Madam," he said, "it's obvious that you've never heard an elephant fart."

My Dad was doing a crossword puzzle and told me that he was struggling to think of another word for stitching.
I said "Hmm, is that sew?"

How do you kill a circus?
Go for the juggler.

A man goes to a zoo and there is only one dog
It was a shitzu.

Before I got through to Seaworld, I had to say: "Jump through the hoop! Do a flip!"
They said my call may be recorded for training porpoises.

A chicken walks into a bar and the bartender says, "Sorry, we don't serve poultry."
The chicken says, "That's OK, I just want a drink."

(1) GRAEME SOUNESS

On only his second home appearance for Liverpool, Souness scored a belter against Manchester United. People may not have known it just then, but in that moment a club legend was born.

In his six years at Liverpool, Souness won 15 major trophies - including the European Cup. Three times.

Uncompromising? Check. Occasionally controversial on and off the pitch? Check. But, under pressure, he had that ability to seemingly stay calm where more hot-headed players would dive in. And, unlike more one-dimensional hard men, Souness backed up all the toughness with cultured ability. Once described as: 'A bear of a player with the delicacy of a violinist,' Souness was an exceptional player who stood out in an exceptional Liverpool team.

Any of you who have had the privilege of seeing me boss the midfield for my local team will know that I have a certain, shall we say 'uncompromising' style to my football. Actually, in fairness, 'brutal' would probably be more accurate.

Anyway, it should come as no surprise that I like to hand it out a bit. Football might be the beautiful game but if you were to find yourself standing between yours truly and a chance to score a wonder goal that will earn me the appreciation, adoration and – let's be honest – free drinks from my team mates, you're in all sorts of trouble.

So, as an homage to those hardy souls who play proper football the way I think it should be played, here's my pick of football's hardest men...

(2) STUART PEARCE

Being hard doesn't just mean dishing it out, you have to take it as well.

Terry Butcher may have played soaked in his own blood, but even he didn't try to run off a broken leg.

That feat of sheer toughness/madness was attempted by Stuart Pearce when playing at the grand old age of 37. A talisman for club and country, Pearce's ability to pick himself up after hard knocks wasn't just limited to physical challenges.

Others would have gone into hiding after missing a World Cup semi-final penalty, but when Pearce exorcised his Turin ghosts during the heady summer of Euro '96, the nation rightly cheered that little bit louder when Pearce's spot kick hit the back of the net.

(3) BILLY BREMNER

The Sunday Times (not a paper I read, personally, but each to their own) described Bremner as: '10st of barbed wire.' While on the smaller side, few players brought his commitment, tenacity, tackling, passing ability and stamina. Plus he scored goals - crucial ones, too - as his four semi-final winners will testify to.

(4) RON HARRIS

Ron 'Chopper' Harris. You could, and should, probably leave it there. Not everyone's cup of tea, Harris was the master of the late tackle and those of you who prefer to keep football beautiful might not always have appreciated the fairness of his approach. Won games for his team though, and ultimately that is what it is all about.

(6) DAVE MACKAY

There were bigger, taller players but, pound-for-pound, Mackay was one of the hardest men to play the game. If you were ever on the wrong end of a Mackay tackle (Note - there is no right end, unless you happened to be Dave Mackay) then you stayed tackled. Even hard men like Billy Bremner were intimidated by him, and that's saying something.

(8) VINNIE JONES

From building sites to Hollywood movies via an FA Cup winning football career, Vinnie Jones had everything a hard man needs - guts, determination and balls - even if they weren't always his own. Add to that the fact that Jones had a slightly unhinged streak that set him out from his compatriots, even in the infamous Wimbledon Crazy Gang - and you have a no-arguments inductee to my Top 10.

(5) ROY KEANE

One of a rare breed of modern era hard men at a time when the demands of a growing international audience meant the game was moving away from tackles that might be described as 'reducers' or 'levellers.' Don't be seduced entirely by the hard man image, though - Keane could play football with the best of them and wasn't just there to dish it out. Although he did. Lots.

(9) NORMAN HUNTER

"Norman bites yer legs" read the fans banner, and few who saw him play would disagree with his inclusion in my list - even if his methods were always a bit unconventional (if you don't know, ask Mick Channon). Hunter by name though… Norman was one pillar of a central defensive unit that underpinned the Leeds side who dominated English football in the late 1960s and early 1970s.

(7) TOMMY SMITH

If it didn't exist already then someone would have had to invent the word 'solid' just to describe Tommy Smith. Bill Shankly summed it up perfectly: 'Tommy doesn't tackle opponents, so much as break them down for resale as scrap.' Born within sight of the ground, the moniker, 'The Anfield Iron' pretty much says it all.

(10) TERRY BUTCHER

Played at the heart of the English defence for a decade - and immortalised by that iconic image of him soaked in his own blood after a World Cup qualifier against Sweden. With a head wound that required stitches, Butcher played on - heading the ball and constantly re-opening the wound. Tough? Few tougher.

LOOK BACK WITH ANDY

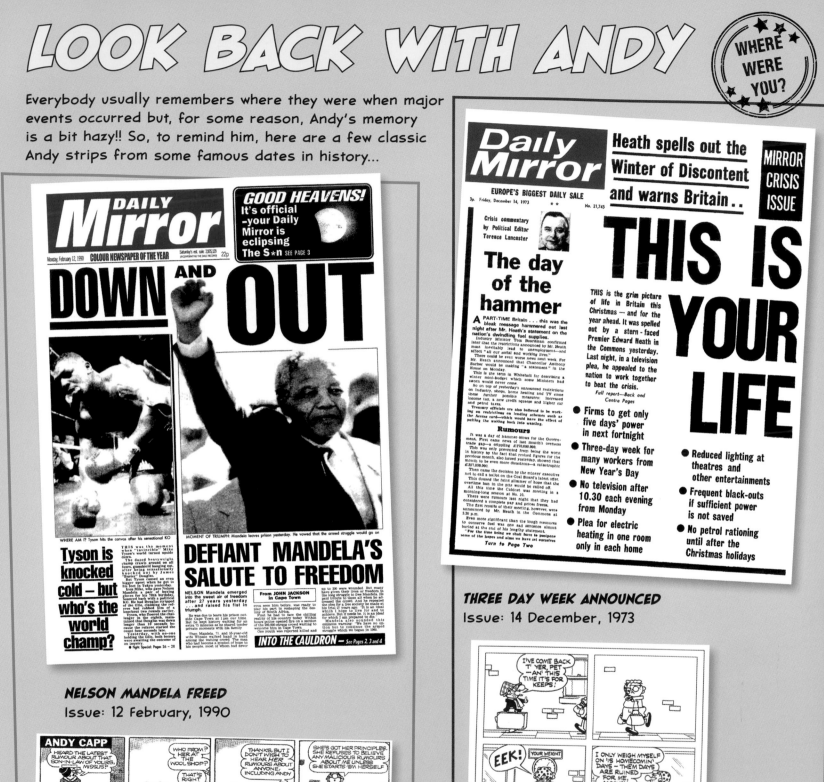

WHERE WERE YOU?

Everybody usually remembers where they were when major events occurred but, for some reason, Andy's memory is a bit hazy!! So, to remind him, here are a few classic Andy strips from some famous dates in history...

NELSON MANDELA FREED
Issue: 12 February, 1990

THREE DAY WEEK ANNOUNCED
Issue: 14 December, 1973

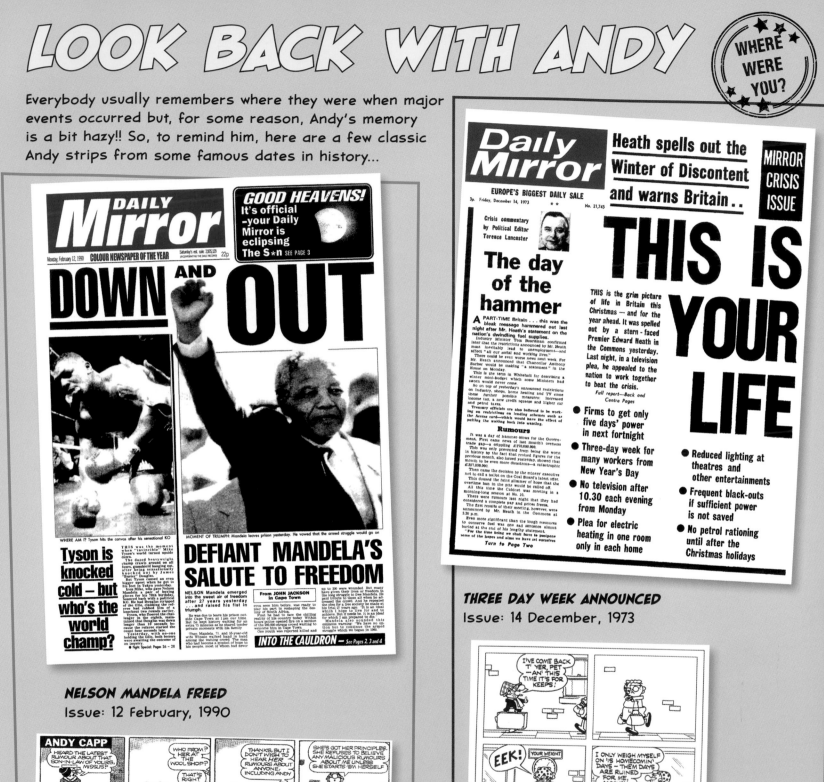

DOWN

1 Devoted to pleasure (9)
2 Unit of surface area (7)
3 Specialist regiment of the British army (inits) (1,1,1)
4 _____ the Peril, cartoon strip (5)
5 Tear (3)
6 Answer a question (5)
7 River that runs through Washington DC (7)
8 Wander from a direct course (5)
12 Type of fruit (5)
14 Covered the inner surface of (5)
18 Sharp vibrating sound (5)
19 White heron (5)
20 Damage the reputation of (9)
22 Tanned animal skin (7)
24 First month (7)
25 Grizzly _____, large North American carnivores (5)
26 Deserve (5)
27 Similar (5)
30 Small soft loaf of bread (3)
32 Organ of sight (3)

ACROSS

1 One's fundamental values (5)
4 Types of mathematical charts (3,6)
9 Tooth at the front of the mouth (7)
10 Musical celebrity (3,4)
11 Take away weapons (5)
13 Informal term for money (5)
15 Month after April (3)
16 Adam and ___ (3)
17 Language of ancient Rome (5)
19 Spanish hero of the 12th century (2,3)
21 Synthetic fabric (5)
23 Viper common in northern Eurasia (5)
24 Sauce made from meat juices (3)
25 Woman's undergarment (3)
26 Molten rock (5)
28 Lotion for refreshing the skin (5)
29 Official language of Ethiopia (7)
31 Emerald Isle (7)
33 Comprehensible (9)
34 Country of north-east Africa (5)

Andy's CrossWord

ANDY SWEARING AGAIN IS NOTHING NEW, BUT THIS IS AN ALTOGETHER DIFFERENT CROSSWORD. COMPLETE THE PUZZLE AND THE GREEN BOXES WILL REVEAL A WELL KNOW ANDY CAPP CHARACTER.

JUNE

MONDAY

1

TUESDAY

2

WEDNESDAY

3

THURSDAY

4

FRIDAY

5

SATURDAY

6

SUNDAY

7

MONDAY

8

TUESDAY

9

WEDNESDAY

10

THURSDAY

11

FRIDAY

12

SATURDAY

13

SUNDAY

14

MONDAY

15

TUESDAY

16

THINGS TO DO

WEDNESDAY

17

THURSDAY

18

FRIDAY

19

SATURDAY

20

SUNDAY

21

MONDAY

22

TUESDAY

23

WEDNESDAY

24

THURSDAY

25

FRIDAY

26

SATURDAY

27

SUNDAY

28

MONDAY

29

TUESDAY

30

SPORTING EVENTS TO KEEP AN EYE OUT FOR
Horse Racing – Epsom Derby Meeting – 5th June to 6th June
Football – UEFA Champions League Final – 6th June
Football – FIFA Women's World Cup 2015 – 6th June to 6th July
Horse Racing – Royal Ascot – 16th June – 20th June
Golf – US Open Championship – 18th June to 21st June
Tennis – Wimbledon – 29th June to 12th July

ANDY'S GUIDE TO FILM AND TV

When you spend as much time on the sofa as me, you get to know a thing or two about TV programmes and films. I've watched all sorts – some brilliant, many awful and others so cringe-worthy I've had to call Flo in from the kitchen or wash-house to switch the flippin' telly off. Here's what I think of some of the stuff, past and present, on the box...

SOAPS We may all moan, or laugh, about these sorts of shows, but flippin' 'eck we don't half spend an awful lot of time talking about them down the pub.

> THAT'S COS THEIR OWN LIVES ARE SO DULL THE ONLY WAY THEY CAN GET A BIT OF EXCITEMENT IS BY GOSSIPING ABOUT IMAGINARY PEOPLE AND FAR-FETCHED PLOTLINES.

THE SIMPSONS Ah, Homer, now he is a man after me own heart, like. He spends a lot of time boozing and getting into trouble. And Bart, well, he could be a mini-me.

> I'VE NEVER HEARD SOMEONE PRAISE A CARTOON CHARACTER SO MUCH. AND I WISH HE'D STOP ASKING ME WHY I COULDN'T BE MORE LIKE FLAMIN' MARGE.

APOCALYPSE NOW How could anyone not love this? It's got everything: mad gun battles; crazy characters; lots of helicopters buzzing around and flames everywhere. Proper action film.

LOOKING FOR ERIC A classic film starring the fruitcake Frenchman himself who appears in a bloke's drug-addled mind to give him advice as his life falls apart. At least I think that's what it was about. I'd had a few drinks when I turned on and was expecting to see lots of football clips.

COOKERY PROGRAMMES Believe it or not, I don't mind these sort of shows. I often watch in envy as they cook up delicious meals then have a little mental bet with mesel' about how badly Flo is going to mess it all up.

THE MAGIC ROUNDABOUT Oh, how I wish they'd bring this back. It was only for five flippin' minutes but was packed with entertainment. A spaced-out hippy rabbit, a bossy snail, a manic dog, a pink cow and a spring with a head and moustache that told everyone to go to bed.

> I THINK HE STILL SEES THOSE CHARACTERS ON THE WAY HOME FROM THE PUB AFTER A GALLON OF BEER.

PSYCHO I've probably seen this movie a dozen times but I still jump out of my skin at the scene where the woman gets bumped off in the shower. And Anthony Perkins pretending to be his dead mum and putting on her voice still has me rolling off the sofa in stitches.

THE GOOD, THE BAD AND THE UGLY You can't beat a spaghetti western. This has all the elements of a classic. Gunfights, horses, desert and blistering sun. Clint Eastwood is fantastic, he's so cool and rugged he reminds me of myself.

> COOL? RUGGED? HE HAS A BIT OF STUBBLE WHEN HE COMES DOWNSTAIRS UNSHAVEN, HUNGOVER, GRUMPY AND WALKING VERY SLOWLY BUT THAT'S AS CLOSE AS HE COMES TO RESEMBLING CLINT EASTWOOD.

TERMINATOR Robot comes back from the future to try to kill a woman who is carrying the baby that will turn into its enemy. Brilliant. And the scenes where you think Arnie Schwarzenegger's Cyborg has finally been finished off but it just pops back up again and starts chasing folk are brilliant... and a bit scary.

FAWLTY TOWERS Top comedy, this. Basil Fawlty is a man who manages to annoy just about everybody that passes through his hotel. Something Jack says I manage to do to every customer who passes through his pub.

YES, INCLUDING HIS OWN WIFE, FLO. A BIT LIKE BASIL FAWLTY. SEE, I REST MY CASE.

SINGING IN THE RAIN Gene Kelly was OK, but that Debbie Reynolds – cor, she was a beauty. She reminded me of a lass I used to fancy who worked at the Riveter's Arms and gave me free pints. I used to be singing in the rain on the way home, with happiness. Until Flo found out. Then I was left out in the rain till she flippin' well calmed down.

DAD'S ARMY Me and Flo used to well crease up watching this (and still do when it comes back on those obscure satellite channels that seem to repeat loads of old comedies). Classic Home Guard funny. Watching Corporal Jones doing everything on the drill a split-second behind his comrades reminds me of Chalkie in our Army days.

AT LEAST I DIDN'T FALL ASLEEP IN THE SENTRY BOX THE DAY THE GENERAL DECIDED TO VISIT THE BASE, LIKE A CERTAIN PRIVATE CAPP DID. AND THE OFFICER WASN'T BEST PLEASED WHEN HE FOUND FOUR EMPTY BEER BOTTLES IN THE SENTRY BOX AND A FILLED-UP CROSSWORD BOOK.

YES MINISTER AND YES PRIME MINISTER These were the shows those bloomin' politicians didn't want us to see cos they gave us a comical glimpse into the inner workings of Parliament and the civil service. Mind you, I still don't really know what the 'eck goes on in the corridors of power, but I had a good laugh trying to find out by watching these programmes.

BACK TO THE FUTURE Another time-travel film, this time a comedy. I loved the mad prof-type bloke in this and his wild enthusiasm. And the bit where Michael J Fox plays Chuck Berry guitar riffs at a college gig long before the singer was even born was a classic moment.

LOCK, STOCK AND TWO SMOKING BARRELS I always love to have a laugh at Cockney wide boys trying to out Cockney each other. This is a movie involving four pals up to their eyeballs in debt to an East End gang boss who try to stitch up some rivals. It all gets very messy, especially when a pair of antique shotguns go missing in a separate incident.

SHAMELESS This was right up my street. It was set mostly in a pub and in the home of some layabout with a load of kids who lived his life in a permanent stupor. It was a proper dys.. dysfun.. dys.. – aah, whatever that word is that means something's not working properly – family. Bit like some of the ones that live in my street.

SET MOSTLY IN A PUB AND THE HOME OF SOME LAYABOUT. WHO DOES THAT REMIND YOU OF, FOLKS?

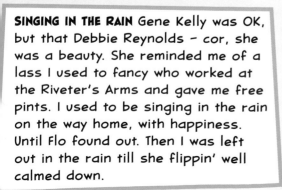

CHALKIE'S CHUCKLES

A sweet little girl is out in the back garden, digging a big deep hole.
A neighbour looks over the fence and says: "Why are you digging that big deep hole?"
"My goldfish died," the sweet little girl says, with a sob.
"I'm really sorry to hear that," the neighbour says,
"but why such a big deep hole for a goldfish?"
The little girl gives him an evil look.
"Because it's inside your cat."

A fellow walks into a bar with a giraffe and they sit down on two stools at the front. The guy says to the barman: "Two beers please, barman."
So he pours them two beers and the giraffe grabs his and drinks it down in one go and his mate follows suit. The guy then says again, "Another two beers please, barman." So the bartender pours two more beers and, once again, the giraffe necks his and his friend does likewise. This goes on for a fair while with the giraffe and his companion downing beer after beer after beer.
The two have had about 17 beers each when the guy looks over at the giraffe who is starting to wobble on his stool... His wobbling gets worse and worse and, eventually, he just passes out and falls backwards off the stool and onto the floor.
The guy looks at him and then gets up off his stool and starts walking out of the bar.
The barman then yells at the guy as he is leaving: "Oi..you can't leave that lyin' there." The man looks at the giraffe and then replies, "That's not a lion that's a giraffe," and walks out.

A police officer sees a woman driving and knitting at the same time.
He yells, "Pull over!"
"No officer," she shouts back, "it's a scarf."

The marriage counselor asked her client, "Did you wake up grumpy this morning?"
"No, I let him sleep in."

It's dinnertime on an airplane. The flight attendant asks an economy passenger if he would like dinner. "What are my choices?" he asks. "Yes or no," she replies.

Q: What's the definition of an accountant?
A: Someone who solves a problem you didn't know you had, in a way you won't ever understand.

Patient: Doctor, doctor. I've come out in spots like cherries on a cake. Doctor: Ah, you must have analogy.

WHAT WERE THEY THINKING FASHION

CHARLIE GEORGE
The iconic image of Charlie George I'd like to remember is the one of him lying flat on the ground after scoring the winner against Liverpool in the 1971 FA Cup Final. What a moment! However, sadly the image I'm actually going to remember from now on is this one. Apparently he was dressed up for a shoot with The Daily Mirror as a pop star. What we don't know though, is why. Answers on a postcard...

When you're a celebrity like yours truly you occasionally get asked to do things that, in modern speak, would be described as 'out of your comfort zone'.

I remember one particular PR stunt when I was asked to turn out for the Hartlepool League of Pigeon Fanciers on the day that our local energy firm was opening their new state of the art wind farm in the same village. Feather's flew that day, I can tell you.

Still, pros like myself usually know where to draw the line. It's a shame that the same couldn't be said of these fellas...

ALLY McCOIST
Whoa! Somebody call the fashion cops – I have no idea why Ally McCoist is dressed as a US police officer but I can say with complete certainty that a crime was definitely being committed when this picture was taken. A crime against fashion, that is.

GAZZA
What a player! Gazza lit-up the 1990 World Cup with his unique skills and, although he ultimately didn't win the cup for England, he did win the nation's hearts with his daft as a brush antics. But a brush was exactly what he needed when sporting these long flowing locks. You'd be forgiven for thinking that Gazza wore them for a laugh, but apparently he actually liked his new hairdo. Didn't last though, thankfully...

GEORGE BEST

The player who had it all – including that great anecdote with the punchline: "Where did it all go wrong?". Well, maybe the answer was round about the time he agreed to dress up as pop star, Boy George. OK, I get the connection in the name, but after that I'm stumped. Still, each to their own...

ASHLEY COLE

Ashley Cole, undoubtedly one of England's greatest ever full backs and a truly world class player. But he scored a bit of an own goal with this publicity shot for the National Lottery. I think the point is to say that win the lottery and like Ashley you can have it all – the looks, the pop-star wife, the Rolls Royce. But if winning the lottery means I have to abandon all good taste and wear clothes that bad I think I'd rather stay on the breadline. And someone really should turn the engine off on that car before they all start choking...

THE ENTIRE LIVERPOOL FA CUP FINAL SQUAD, 1996

If a footballer is lucky enough to be involved in an FA Cup final, the day of the big match must hold quite a few terrors. All that pressure, the greater than usual expectation of the crowd and the massive TV audience. In fact, amidst all of that probably the easiest thing to get right is the walk about on the Wembley pitch before kick-off. Usually, anyway. Not for Liverpool in '96 though – somehow, thanks to their choice of suits, they managed to turn a simple walk in the park into one of the most memorable footballing, 'What were they thinking?' moments of all time.

LOOK BACK WITH ANDY

Everybody usually remembers where they were when major events occurred but, for some reason, Andy's memory is a bit hazy!! So, to remind him, here are a few classic Andy strips from some famous dates in history...

MARGARET THATCHER ELECTED PRIME MINISTER
Issue: 4 May, 1979

HUMAN DNA GENOME MAPPED
Issue: 27 June, 2000

JACK'S PUB QUIZ

SPORTS

1. What type of sporting event is held at Fontwell, Pontefract and Ripon?

2. In which sport would players stand behind the 'oche'?

3. In cricket, what are leg byes and no-balls known as?

4. Which is the only non-English football team to have won the FA Cup?

5. In which sport does this sequence occur: red, blue, white, black, orange and black & white?

6. In which position did former England rugby union captain, Martin Johnson, play?

7. Which English football club is nicknamed the 'Black Cats'?

8. Which golf club is known as the 'Home of Golf'?

9. How many balls are on the table at the start of a game of snooker?

10. What do Terry Venables, Glenn Hoddle and Kevin Keegan have in common?

11. In which year did London last host the summer Olympic Games?

12. Who was the last British man to win the Wimbledon men's singles title before Andy Murray triumphed in 2013?

JULY

WEDNESDAY

1

_____

THURSDAY

2

_____

FRIDAY

3

_____

SATURDAY

4

_____

SUNDAY

5

_____

MONDAY

6

_____

TUESDAY

7

_____

WEDNESDAY

8

THURSDAY

9

_____

FRIDAY

10

_____

SATURDAY

11

_____

SUNDAY

12

_____

MONDAY

13

Bank Holiday (Northern Ireland)

_____

TUESDAY

14

_____

WEDNESDAY

15

_____

THURSDAY

16

THINGS TO DO

FRIDAY

17

SATURDAY

18

SUNDAY

19

MONDAY

20

TUESDAY

21

WEDNESDAY

22

THURSDAY

23

FRIDAY

24

SATURDAY

25

SUNDAY

26

MONDAY

27

TUESDAY

28

WEDNESDAY

29

THURSDAY

30

FRIDAY

31

SPORTING EVENTS TO KEEP AN EYE OUT FOR
Cycling – Tour de France begins – 5th July
Cricket – England v Australia 1st Ashes Test Match – 8th July to 12th July
Golf – The 144th Open Championship – 16th July to 19th July
Cricket – England v Australia 2nd Ashes Test Match – 16th July to 20th July
Cricket – England v Australia 3rd Ashes Test Match – 29th July to 2nd August
Horse Racing – Glorious Goodwood

DON'T COP IT

ANDY IS ON HIS WAY TO MEET CHALKIE FOR A GAME OF POOL. HOWEVER, THE LOCAL PLOD WANT TO SPEAK TO HIM ABOUT THAT UNFORTUNATE INCIDENT AT THE PUB LAST NIGHT.

WHICH PATH KEEPS ANDY AWAY FROM THE COPS?

ANDY'S GUIDE TO SUMMER HOLIDAYS

There's nowt like a summer's day. Me and Flo are off on our hols to the seaside soon. I love strolling along the prom with the whiff of fish 'n' chips in the air, lazing on a deck chair with a can by me side and trying out new boozers by the beach (luckily Flo's just been paid so I can stop in them a bit longer). Here's my advice on how to have a great holiday...

SUN Believe it or not, it does come out in England – sometimes. As soon as I see the sun, I grab a few cans and head for the beach. Flo gets a bit narked with all the empties lying around our deck chairs, but it helps me find my spot when I pop back from the offie with more booze.

> I WASN'T TOO HAPPY WHEN I WENT FOR A STROLL AND CAME BACK TO FIND SOME PESKY KIDS HAD BUILT A SANDCASTLE NEXT TO ANDY AS HE SNOOZED AND USED ALL HIS CANS AS TOWERS.

FOOD Ye cannot beat seaside fish suppers. I don't know what it is but they always taste better when yer on holiday. Maybe the ones at my local chippy are just rubbish (I'm usually so sozzled, I don't care) but the ones ye get at resorts are smashing. Ye must try 'em.

> THEY PROBABLY TASTE A LOT BETTER COS I ALWAYS END UP FLIPPIN' PAYING FOR THEM.

SAND Great for building castles with if yer a kid, but a right pain if ye have fish 'n' chips or beer on the beach. Best thing is to eat before you get there and buy those really tall cans or bottles so they stick so far up out of the sand it won't get to the bit you drink from.

SEA As you well know, the waters around Britain are flamin' freezing even in the height of summer, so going for a swim is not most people's idea of fun. However, a paddle can be quite invigorating and the cold air coming off the sea helps keep your beer chilled.

> INVIGORATING? I DON'T THINK I'VE EVER HEARD ANYONE YELP SO PATHETICALLY WHEN THEY DIP THEIR TOES IN THE WATER BEFORE RUSHING BACK TO HIS DECK CHAIR.

PUBS I just love sitting watching the sun go down with a pint in yer hand at a lovely boozer by the beach. After a hard day lying around on a deck chair, why not pop to the bar for a night cap?

> I'VE HEARD HIS NIGHTCAPS START AT AROUND 5PM AND GO ON TILL CLOSING TIME.

AMUSEMENTS Most seaside towns have slot machine arcades where I often while away the time spending Flo's loose change. I've been known to have a little winner, or three, on the one-armed bandits. Although carting all that cash around can be a bit of a flamin' pain so I tend to put it back in. That prolongs the fun.

RAIN Of course, there's always going to be a downpour when you're on your jollies, England wouldn't be England without it. Luckily there are plenty of indoor things to do at most resorts, such as pool, snooker, gambling at bookies, darts, watching the telly in pubs and drinking. So don't be put off by a bit of rain.

> AND HE ALWAYS TELLS ME HE DOES LOTS OF DIFFERENT THINGS WHEN HE GOES AWAY.

CHALKIE'S CHUCKLES

One day three women went to the top of a helter skelter at the fairground.

There was a black haired, brown haired, and a blonde haired woman.

When they got to the top a genie appeared from nowhere and said, "It's your lucky day! When you're going down the ride, shout out the one thing that you want and lo! you will land in it at the bottom."

So the black haired woman went down and shouted, "Money!" and landed in a load of cash.

The brown haired woman went down and shouted, "Gorgeous men!" and landed in a pile of male models.

The blonde woman wasn't listening to the genie so she went down shouting, "Weeeeeee!"

What do you get when you cross poison ivy and a four leaf clover? A rash of good luck!

Did you hear about the red ship and the blue ship that collided? Both crews were marooned.

A man was having trouble with his parrot swearing and a friend told him to put the parrot in the fridge for a while as a punishment.

The man told his parrot he would do this and the next time it swore he duly put it in the fridge. Later he took the parrot out and it turned back to look in the fridge and said "What did the chicken do?"

Doctor Clarke always stopped at his local pub after work for a hazelnut daiquiri [a special drink the bartender created jus for him].

One day, Dermot, the barman ran out of hazelnut flavour so h substituted hickory nuts instead

Doctor Clarke took one sip of the drink and exclaimed: "This isn't a hazelnut daiquiri. Dermot!"

"No, I'm sorry," replied Dermot "It's a hickory daiquiri, doc."

"Read all about it!" yelled the newsboy, hawking his newspapers on the corner.
"Fifty people swindled! Fifty people swindled!"
Curious, a businessman bought a paper. "Hey," he said. "There's nothing in here about 50 people being swindled."
"Read all about it!" yelled the newsboy again.
"Fifty-one people swindled!"

Will was trying to teach his young son the evils of alcohol. He put one worm in a glass of water and another worm in a glass of whisky. The worm in the water lived, while the one in the whisky curled up and died.
"All right, son," said Will. "What does that show you?"
"Well, Dad, it shows that if you drink alcohol, you will not have worms."

ASK ANDY

GOT A PROBLEM? CONSIDER IT SOLVED!

Dear Andy,

I've noticed that when you go fishing you never seem to catch much. Have you thought about taking up a different hobby?

Cheryl, London.

ANDY'S REPLY

Well, Cheryl, pet, you're right, it does look like I rarely get a bite. But there's so much more to fishing than actually catching the flippin' things. There's the tranquility of just me and a case of beer, with no one to nag me about drinking too flamin' much. Then there's the camaraderie with yer fellow anglers – in my case it usually consists of them telling me how many bloomin' fish they've got while I stare at an empty basket. But this actually gives me a much deeper sense of satisfaction when I do land one.

Dear Andy,

My girlfriend's cooking is awful but I don't have the heart to tell her. As a result I end up having to shovel her meals down my throat while trying not to gag, or rushing out of the room to spit it out in a dustbin. I'm afraid she'll catch me one day and dump me.

Have you any advice to help me out of this tricky situation?

Eric, Newhaven.

ANDY'S REPLY

Flippin' 'eck Eric, yer in a right spot of bother there, lad, and you have my full sympathy. Well, ye'v got a few choices. You can pretend yer not hungry and tell your lass ye'v just popped round fer a drink. That way ye don't upset her and ye don't have to eat her muck. Then, later, on the way home or when ye pop out to the pub, get yersel some fish 'n' chips or a kebab. Another choice is to do what I do and be honest. I frequently tell Flo her cooking's rubbish. But that's not without its danger, I often end up wearing my dinner as a result. Yer other choice is to get a new girlfriend, one who can cook.

Dear Andy,

My girlfriend wants to go abroad on holiday but I hate the sun and all that funny food. She says I'm not very adventurous and she might be right. I don't want to lose her so do you reckon you could give me some advice on how to play this?

Brendan, Swansea.

ANDY'S REPLY

Brendan, lasses seem to love exotic stuff for some reason and they always seem t'think that means going abroad. I've taken Flo to the coast in England for as long as I can remember (alright, she pays, but I come up with the locations) and we have yet to have a bad holiday. (Not counting the one where I got locked out of the B&B, had to sleep in the shed and woke up covered in snails). Just tell yer lass that this day and age you can have all the exotic stuff here – Greece and Turkey? Kebab shops all over Britain. Spain? Tapas bars in every town. Italy? Pizza joints galore. And tell her ye'll save a fortune on the air fare, meaning ye can spend a bucket load on booze, food and down the amusement arcades. And if yer really lucky, it'll be sunny for at least one day. If not, there's always the bingo, the pub and the eat-in chippy.

JACK'S PUB QUIZ

MOVIE SPECIAL

1. What is the name of the golden robot in the Star Wars films?

2. What nationality is the actress Penelope Cruz, star of 'Vicky Cristina Barcelona'?

3. Which ex-footballer successfully acted in movies such as 'Mean Machine'?

4. The Phelps twins, James and Oliver, starred in which series of films?

5. What nationality is film director, Bernardo Bertolucci?

6. Which American directed the film 'Django Unchained'?

7. Which character did the actor, Rupert Everett, voice in the film 'Shrek the Third'?

8. What is the nationality of the actress and director, Sophie Marceau?

9. Sean Connery plays a reclusive author in which 2000 movie?

10. Which character does Michael Caine play in 'The Dark Knight Rises'?

11. Who is Tom Cruise's character in the 'Mission: Impossible' series of movies?

12. Which actor played Reuben Tishkoff in the film 'Ocean's Thirteen'?

13. What is unusual about John Travolta's role in the film musical 'Hairspray'?

14. Which English actress starred in the 2011 film 'Love, Wedding, Marriage'?

15. Which actor co-starred with Emma Thompson in the film 'Love Actually'?

16. Which well-known actress starred in the 2002 film 'Panic Room'?

17. Which American actor and comedian starred in the film 'Girl Walks into a Bar'?

18. Which American actress starred in the film 'Love Happens'?

19. Who co-starred with Meryl Streep in the comedy film 'Hope Springs'?

20. Who was Kristen Stewart's co-star in the film 'The Twilight Saga'?

21. Whose films have included 'Schindler's List' and 'Taken'?

22. What character did Rupert Grint play in the Harry Potter series of movies?

23. Who starred as Maria in the Oscar-winning musical 'The Sound of Music'?

24. Danny Boyle won the Academy Award for Best Director in 2009 for which film?

25. Who was Angelina Jolie's co-star in the film 'Mr. And Mrs. Smith'?

LOOK BACK WITH ANDY

Everybody usually remembers where they were when major events occurred but, for some reason, Andy's memory is a bit hazy!! So, to remind him, here are a few classic Andy strips from some famous dates in history...

CUBAN MISSILE CRISIS
Issue: 23 October, 1962

ENGLAND WIN THE 2005 ASHES
Issue: 13 September, 2005

WHERE WERE YOU?

Andy's CrossWord

CAN YOU COMPLETE THIS PUZZLING CROSSWORD? FILL IN THE CLUES AND THE GREEN BOXES WILL REVEAL A WELL KNOW ANDY CAPP CHARACTER...

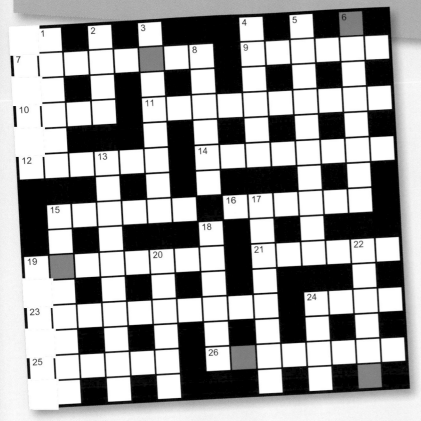

DOWN

1 Workers who extract ore or minerals from the earth (6)
2 Certificate given for a basic level subject taken in school (1,1,1,1)
3 Relating to the brain (8)
4 Rich cake (6)
5 Descends steeply and rapidly (aircraft) (5,5)
6 Played boisterously (8)
8 Liveliness of mind or spirit (6)
13 Combat airman (10)
15 Non-commissioned army rank (8)
17 Sub-atomic particle (8)
18 Symbol of social disgrace (6)
20 Outwardly (6)
22 A collection of star systems (6)
24 Ring of light around the head of an angel or saint (4)

ACROSS

7 Distinct in form or concept (8)
9 Out of one's own country (6)
10 Outdoor festival (4)
11 Saying (10)
12 Line on a weather map (6)
14 Overwhelm (8)
15 Try out (6)
16 Intensely hot (6)
19 Escape (from prison) (5,3)
21 Emblem flown as a symbol of nationality (6)
23 Heavy motionless burden (4,6)
24 50 per cent (4)
25 Reveal (6)
26 Sudden loss of blood (8)

B!****! ****+^

AUGUST

SATURDAY

1

___

SUNDAY

2

___

MONDAY

3

Bank Holiday (Scotland)
___

TUESDAY

4

___

WEDNESDAY

5

___

THURSDAY

6

___

FRIDAY

7

___

SATURDAY

8

SUNDAY

9

___

MONDAY

10

___

TUESDAY

11

___

WEDNESDAY

12

___

THURSDAY

13

___

FRIDAY

14

___

SATURDAY

15

___

SUNDAY

16

THINGS TO DO

MONDAY

17

TUESDAY

18

WEDNESDAY

19

THURSDAY

20

FRIDAY

21

SATURDAY

22

SUNDAY

23

MONDAY

24

TUESDAY

25

WEDNESDAY

26

THURSDAY

27

FRIDAY

28

SATURDAY

29

SUNDAY

30

MONDAY

31

Bank Holiday (UK except Scotland)

SPORTING EVENTS TO KEEP AN EYE OUT FOR
Cricket – England v Australia 4th Ashes Test Match – 6th August to 10th August
Golf – US PGA Championship – 13th August to 16th August
Cricket – England v Australia 5th Ashes Test Match – 20th August to 24th August
Athletics – World Championships – 22nd August to 30th August
Tennis – US Open – 31st August to 13th September
Football – Start of 2015/2016 Premier League

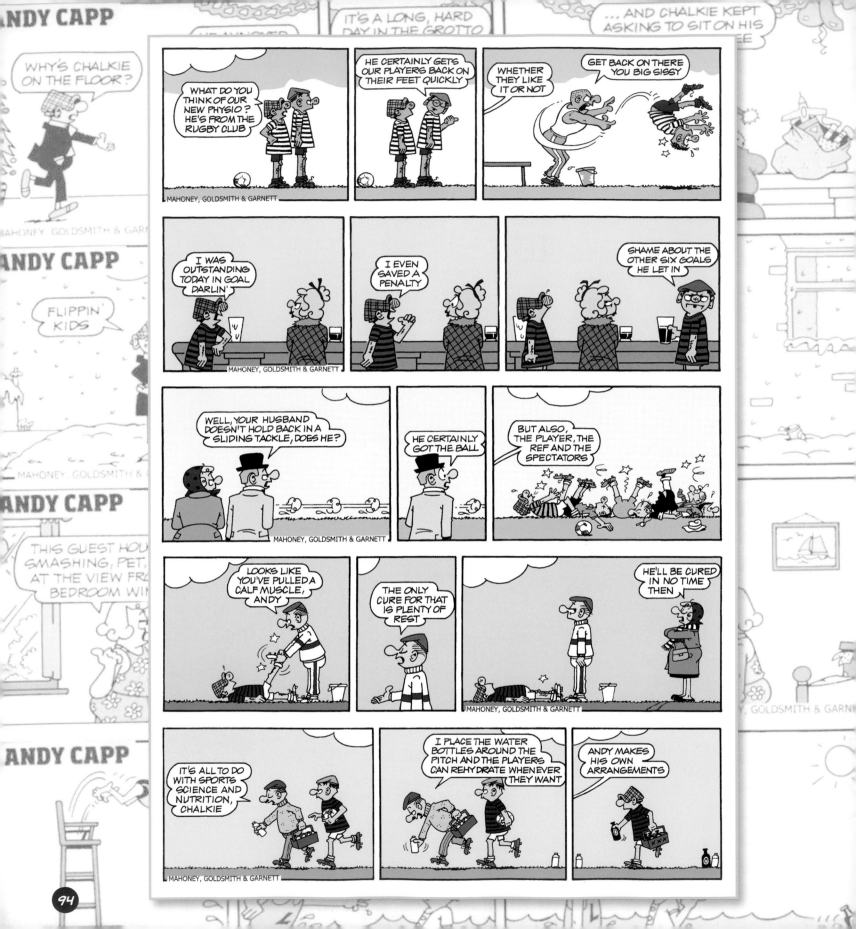

ANDY'S GUIDE TO FOOTBALL

Football. I live it, breathe it and drink before, during and after it. But, astonishingly, there are people who know nothing about the beautiful game. Like Flo. She does come along now and again, but boy does it get bloomin' wearing trying to explain every last thing to her, like offsides and what the blinkin' ref is doing. So, here's my simple guide to the game – for those who haven't quite grasped what's going on...

OFFICIALS When it comes to refs, there's one simple rule. If he gives a decision in your favour, he's spot on and deserves applause. If he blows against you, he's 100% wrong and the worst ref in the world.

PLAYERS You could be forgiven for thinking today's namby pamby stars get shot each week the way they slump to the ground at the merest of touches. But watch in amazement as they are brought round by a combination of deep heat spray and their opponent being booked. Grrrr.

SUPPORTERS Fans can often be heard slagging off their team when they are playing rubbish. This is normal. But if an opposition fan calls the same stars hopeless, don't be surprised to see them being chased down the street by an angry mob.

> USUALLY LED BY ANDY.

MEDICAL STAFF It's difficult for today's physios to know which bit of an injured player to treat – especially as they normally go down holding their face after being kicked, butted or elbowed in the flamin' chest.

MANAGERS If the gaffer brings on subs with your team losing and they end up getting beat, he is a clueless idiot. But if one of those subs scores the winning goal, the boss is a genius who you never doubted.

GOALKEEPERS These are the people who stand at either end of the pitch in different colours to the rest of the team and try to stop goals being scored. They also provide occasional entertainment by acting like flamin' clowns for no apparent reason.

KNOW-ALLS There is always someone who lets you know why the manager is wrong, which players he should have picked, what the striker who's just missed should have done and that the ref doesn't know the rules.

HALF-TIME ENTERTAINMENT Usually kids taking penalties against the mascot, cheerleaders waving their pom poms or a raffle with a top prize of a weekend in Mrs Grimes' B&B.

PROGRAMMES The glossy little booklet that has lots of pictures of the players along with previous results (as if you didn't blinkin' well know). There are also messages from the manager and the captain saying exactly the same blinkin' thing – that we need to win this game. I could flamin' well write that.

FOOD STALLS When you're starving, the grub smells delicious at those stands outside the ground. But if you've been fed, it smells bloomin' vile.

> HE DIDN'T SAY THAT WHEN GREASY JOE OFFERED HIM A FREE BURGER FROM HIS STALL.

CHALKIE'S GUIDE TO ANDY'S TERRACE TALK

At matches you will hear a lot of bad language from the crowd at times. If you sit next to Andy, you'll hear it the entire game.

It is directed at players, refs and opposition supporters. In Andy's case, it is also directed at me if I haven't got the beers in at half time.

It can be difficult to understand what is being said, so I've translated some of Andy's foul mouthed rants for you.

Ref, you ******* useless ******* ****, ******* never a ******* foul you ***. ****** ****. Translation. I think you got that wrong, referee and when you see the replay I have no doubt you will agree.

You fat ******* **** why didn't you ******* lump it ******* ****. You're not ******* Pele. Translation. I think trying to dribble the ball out of defence with your limited footballing skills and surrounded by opposition players was a little unwise. You should really have just booted it away.

Oh ******* **** ref **** **** ******* ****. ******* ****, you useless ******. **** **** ****. Translation: I'm not very happy with that decision.

Six nil? Six ******* nil? What a waste of ******* money you ******* *****. **** **** ****. Translation: I wish I'd stayed in the pub.

I'm ******* parched, Chalkie, where's the ******* drinks you *******, ****** ****** *** ****** *** ****** *** ****** *** ****** ***. Translation: It's your round, Chalkie.

How the ******* ******* did he miss that? ******* ******* *** My hopeless mother-in-law could have scored from there. Translation: That striker's rubbish.

ANDY'S GUIDE TO COMMENTATOR SPEAK

Commentators don't half come out with some drivel during games.

Sometimes I'm convinced they are watching a different match to the rest of us.

All they have to bloomin' well do is look at what's going on and tell you. Even I could manage that, but, oh no, they treat us to their version of events, which can differ wildly from what we are seeing on the box. Here's what I mean...

ANDY – WHAT THEY SAY: The linesman flagged for offside but it looked tight to me.
CHALKIE – WHAT THEY MEAN: He was well offside, but I wanted him to go and score so I could put my excited voice on because this game is pretty boring.

ANDY – WHAT THEY SAY: The Premier League is the best in the world.
JACK – WHAT THEY MEAN: No, it's not, I've watched Spanish football and the Bundesliga and they are way better.

ANDY – WHAT THEY SAY: That win gives England a timely boost going into the World Cup this year.
CHALKIE – WHAT THEY MEAN: It was a friendly against (fill in rubbish opposition) who are not the best in the world, we struggled to score. We haven't got a hope in hell of winning the World Cup.

ANDY – WHAT THEY SAY: The player did well to win the penalty there (usually said when England are playing or English clubs are in Europe).
JACK – WHAT THEY MEAN: He dived.

ANDY – WHAT THEY SAY: San Marino may be a small team on the world stage, but you can never take them lightly, they work hard for each other and play with pride and passion.
CHALKIE – WHAT THEY MEAN: They are rubbish. A bunch of part-timers who are mostly fishermen and train once a week. If you can't beat them you really are in trouble.

ANDY – WHAT THEY SAY: You have to wonder what's going through the manager's mind there as his team trail five nil.
JACK – WHAT THEY MEAN: He hasn't a clue what he's doing.

ANDY – WHAT THEY SAY: It's the magic of the FA Cup, you never know what might happen here with Woking against Manchester United.
CHALKIE – WHAT THEY MEAN: Woking have not got a hope.

ANDY – WHAT THEY SAY: Well, there was minimum contact before he fell to the ground.
JACK – WHAT THEY MEAN: He never touched him.

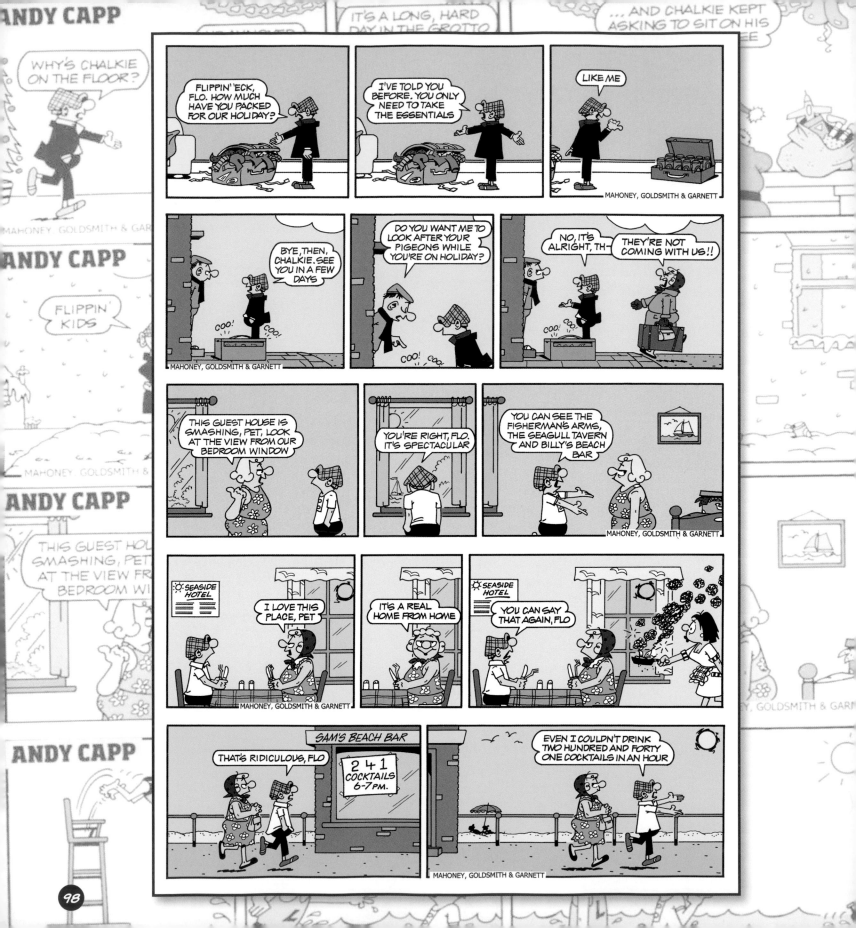

CHALKIE'S CHUCKLES

A man is stranded on a desert island for 10 years. One day a beautiful girl swims to shore in a wetsuit.

Man: "Hi! I am so happy to see you."

Girl: "Hi! It seems like you've been here a long time. How long has it been since you've had a cigarette?"

Man: "It's been 10 years!"

With this information the girl unzips a slot on the arm of her wet suit and gives the man a cigarette.

Man: "Thank you so much!"

Girl: "So tell me how long has it been since you had a drink?"

Man: "It's been 10 years!"

The girl unzips another pocket on her wet suit and comes out with a flask of 12 year old malt whisky and gives the man a drink.

Man: "Thank you so much. You are like a miracle!"

Girl (starting to unzip the front of her wet suit): "So tell me then, how long has it been since you played around?"

Man: "Oh, my God, don't tell me you've got a set of golf clubs in there, too...!"

David was overweight and went to the doc., who told him to eat what he wanted for two days, skip the next day, and eat for the next two days. If he followed that diet, he would lose five pounds in two weeks. One month later, David went back to the doc. who weighed him. David had lost 55 pounds.

The doctor asked David if he was finding it hard to follow the diet. "No," replied David. "But skipping all day nearly kills me!"

A dog goes into the Job Centre and says:"I'm looking for a job"."

The chap behind the counter is amazed that he is looking at a talking dog , but doesn't show it...

"I think I can recommend the very thing," he says.

"There's a circus just about to open for business in the town square. Nip down there and you should be OK."

To which the dog replies.......

"Fine, but why would they want a plumber?"

What do you get when you cross a Karate expert with a pig?

Pork chops!

What clothes does a house wear?
Address.

"Doctor, doctor. I keep having this dream I'm a cowboy."

"That's quite alright, there's quite a bit of that around. How long has it been going on for?"

"About a yee-ha."

A grasshopper walks into a bar and the bartender says: "Hey, we have a drink named after you."
The grasshopper says: "What, you have a drink named Roger?"

LOOK BACK WITH ANDY

Everybody usually remembers where they were when major events occurred but, for some reason, Andy's memory is a bit hazy!! So, to remind him, here are a few classic Andy strips from some famous dates in history...

PRINCE WILLIAM AND CATHERINE MIDDLETON MARRY
Issue: 30 April, 2011

JOHN PROFUMO RESIGNS AS WAR MINISTER
Issue: 6 June, 1963

JACK'S PUB QUIZ

GENERAL KNOWLEDGE

1. How many colours are in a rainbow?

2. What is the UK's second largest city?

3. What is Prince Phillip's royal title?

4. The events of which TV soap take place in, or around, Albert Square?

5. Which nocturnal creature is Britain's largest land carnivore?

6. Which is Britain's highest mountain?

7. The drink, Calvados, is made from which fruit?

8. Who won his only Best Actor Oscar for the 1969 western 'True Grit?'

9. In which year did Margaret Thatcher become British Prime Minister?

10. What was model Katie Price's original celebrity name?

11. What is regarded as London's most popular paid tourist attraction?

12. How are Harry, Zayn, Louis, Niall and Liam collectively known?

SEPTEMBER

TUESDAY

1
_____

WEDNESDAY

2
_____

THURSDAY

3
_____

FRIDAY

4
_____

SATURDAY

5
_____

SUNDAY

6
_____

MONDAY

7
_____

TUESDAY

8

WEDNESDAY

9
_____

THURSDAY

10
_____

FRIDAY

11
_____

SATURDAY

12
_____

SUNDAY

13
_____

MONDAY

14
_____

TUESDAY

15
_____

WEDNESDAY

16

THINGS TO DO

THURSDAY

17

FRIDAY

18

SATURDAY

19

SUNDAY

20

MONDAY

21

TUESDAY

22

WEDNESDAY

23

THURSDAY

24

FRIDAY

25

SATURDAY

26

SUNDAY

27

MONDAY

28

TUESDAY

29

WEDNESDAY

30

THURSDAY

31

THINGS TO DO

SPORTING EVENTS TO KEEP AN EYE OUT FOR
Rugby Union – 2015 Rugby World Cup – 18th September to 31st October
Tennis – US Open – 31st August to 13th September
Horse Racing – St Leger Festival

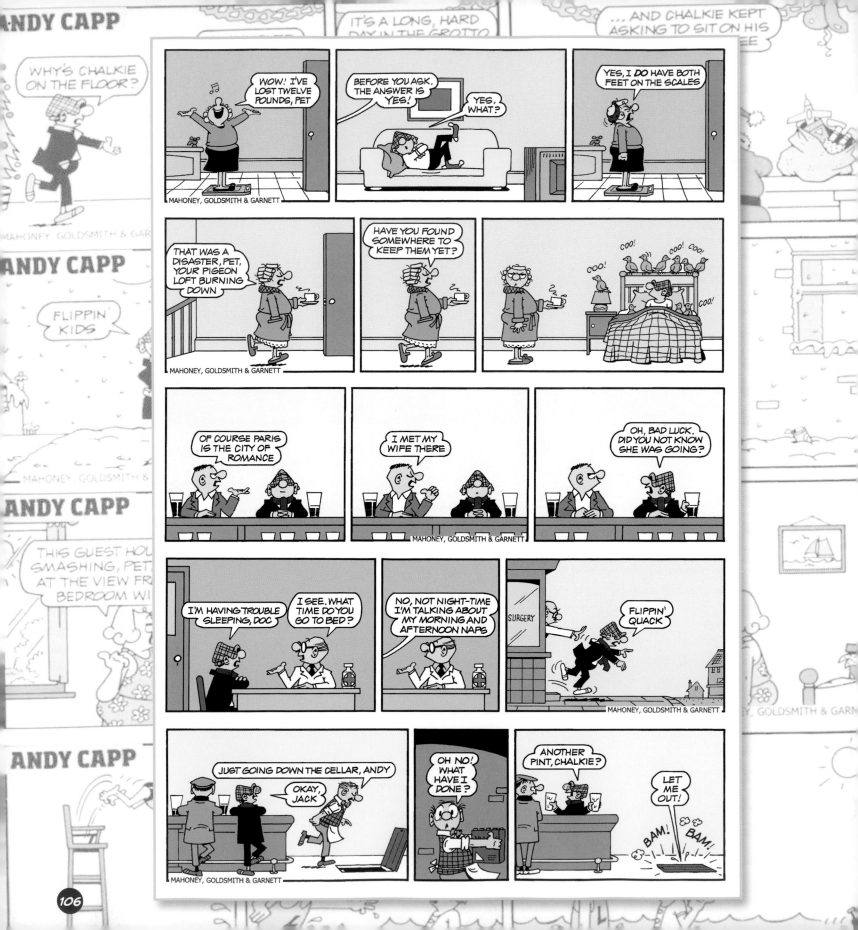

FLO'S KITCHEN

Hello again, folks. Or should I say, "Hola?" Cos today we're going to do a Spanish omelette. This is a really simple, but totally easy, dish and the taste will transport you to those sunny beaches of the Costa del Sol – not that I've ever been there, we can just about afford Whitby for our hols if I work overtime. Anyway for this Iberian experience you need to get yourself a few simple bits and pieces...

INGREDIENTS
500g new potatoes
1 onion, white
150ml extra-virgin olive oil
6 eggs

READY? LET'S GET THOSE PINNIES ON AND LET'S GET OMELETTING...

METHOD:

Peel the potatoes, cut into slices.
Chop the onion.

Heat oil in a large frying pan, add the spuds and onion and cook gently for half an hour, stirring now and again until the potatoes soften. Strain the potatoes and onions and place in a large bowl (put the strained oil to one side).

Beat the eggs, then stir into the spuds. You can add salt and pepper if you fancy. Heat some of the strained oil in another pan. Tip everything into the pan and cook on a moderate heat. Shape the omelette with a spatula.

When almost set, flip onto a plate, slide back into the pan and cook a few more minutes. Flip twice more, cooking the omelette briefly each time and pressing the edges to keep the shape. Slip the omelette onto a plate and cool for 10 minutes before serving.

Well, there you have it amigos. Add a bit of Tabasco sauce if you like it hot and spicy. As they say in Spain, "Disfrutar," which I think means enjoy, even if it sounds like something to do with fruit.

SOMEONE WILL BE WEARING THESE EGGS IF THEY'RE NOT CAREFUL. RIGHT, HERE'S WHAT YOU'LL NEED.

I OFTEN GET SOME CERVEZAS TO MAKE IT A PROPER SPANISH EXPERIENCE – AND DROWN OUT THE TASTE OF BURNT EGGS, HEH HEH.

WHAT'S SPANISH FOR "HOW DID YOU MANAGE TO RUIN A SIMPLE OMELETTE"? HA HA.

ANDY'S GUIDE TO FISHING

Fishing is brilliant! What better way to pass the time of day than relaxing on the riverbank with a case load of beer while waiting for that exciting moment when the line twitches (often a long wait in my case) and you land that catch? Oh yes, some of my best days have been spent alone by the water – usually without even fish for company. And there's often other like-minded folk around to share your tales of the ones that got away. Here's my tips on how to get the most out of fishing...

LEAVE YOUR WIFE AT HOME

The only enjoyment Flo gets out of coming fishing with me is taking the flamin' Mick when I land a tiddler.

> IF I DIDN'T MAKE MY OWN ENTERTAINMENT I'D BE BORED SILLY. AND HE DOES CATCH A LOT OF TIDDLERS.

RELAX

Someone once said: "Even a bad day's fishing is better than a good day of work." I've no idea about the work bit, but angling is a stress-busting activity.

BE PREPARED

You have to be ready for any eventuality. So, I always take a cold box for the beer in case of hot weather, gloves to grip my can with if it's freezing, extra booze in case I stay longer than expected and a radio to keep up with the horse racing.

BE PREPARED FOR BAD WEATHER

Don't get caught out by the rain. Make sure you take a big brolly to stop your booze from being watered down by a sudden shower as you drink.

> ANDY MADE THAT MISTAKE ONCE THEN UPSET JACK BY SAYING THE DILUTED BEER REMINDED HIM OF THE STUFF SERVED AT THE PUB.

ALWAYS EXAGGERATE

Folk'll never believe how big that fish you caught was, only for it to blinkin' escape. So it's best to pretend it was massive.

> I SOMETIMES WONDER IF THE FISH HE BRAGS ABOUT LETTING GO WOULD ACTUALLY FIT IN THAT SMALL RIVER.

DON'T BLAME THE FISH

I've been known to stand on the riverbank yelling obscenities at the water during yet another biting drought. You do look a bit daft.

TAKE PLENTY TO DRINK

You could be by that riverbank for a long time, so make sure you have lots of fluids. But pace yourself, you don't wanna run out of beer before you run out of bait.

SAY NOWT

If you've been out fishing all day and not caught so much as a sprat. Don't tell anyone down the pub. Being honest will only spark a frenzy of Mick-taking.

DON'T TAKE IT PERSONALLY

If the fish are not biting, it's nowt to do with your angling skills. That's what I keep telling meself, anyway. It's purely luck of the draw that you sit there all flamin' day and catch nowt while that smug bloke a few yards down waltzes off home with a basket full.

CHALKIE'S CHUCKLES

A man died and went to Heaven. At the pearly gates he was told: "You really didn't do anything particularly good or bad so we're not sure what to do with you. Can you tell us anything you did that can help us make a decision?" The newly arrived soul replied: "Once I was driving along and came upon a person who was being harassed by a group of thugs. So I pulled over, got out a bat, and went up to the leader of the thugs. He was a big, muscular guy with a ring pierced through his lip. Well, I tore the ring out of his lip, and told him he and his gang had better stop bothering this guy or they would have to deal with me!" "Wow, that's impressive, when did this happen?" "About three minutes ago!"

So I was walking down the road when a car pulls up next to me. The windows winds down, and a voice says: "Son, I'll give you a sweet to get into my car!"

"No!" I said, and walked off.

The car pulls up again.. "Come on, son, I'll give you a football magazine if you'll get in my car!" "NO WAY!"

The car pulls up a third time, and the guy said "Look son, I'll give you any magazine you want, and as many sweets you'd like if you'll get in the car!"

At this point I just got annoyed. "DAD! You bought the Skoda, you live with it!"

A man walks into a bar with a slab of tarmac under his arm and says, "Beer please, and one for the road."

What do you get when you cross a hula dancer with a boxer?
A Hawaiian Punch!

What did one candle say to the other candle?
Let's go out tonight!

What do you call a boomerang that doesn't come back?
A stick.

Q: What has eight eyes and eight legs?
A: Eight pirates.

FOOTIES FOULEST HAIRCUTS

Here at Mirror Towers, the Andy Capp fan club mailbox is literally chock-full of letters – just like this one:

"Dear Andy,
   I've been following your adventures in The Daily Mirror for years and I wanted you to know I think you're brilliant.
   In fact, I think you're so great Flo should give you more money to spend at the pub.

ARE YOU SURE YOU DIDN'T WRITE THIS ANDY?

Just one question, you're always wearing that hat – what does your haircut look like underneath?!"

Well, I've never revealed my hairstyle cos the ladies love me in a hat and it adds to my mysterious nature. Ahem. However, just because I don't reveal my own style doesn't mean I can't comment on other people's – and once again the world of football throws up a few unique examples...

DAVID BECKHAM

Good looking, fabulously talented, great role model and a sure fire hit with the ladies. But enough about me, what about England's David Beckham? All that fame and money must have gone to his head when he sported this look when he signed for Real Madrid. Our Becks has had a few shockers down the years in the hair department – but this one was my least favourite. Too girly for me.

TARIBO WEST

Not sure where to start with this one. On the one hand you got to give it to Taribo West for having the confidence to try this style out – in fact he did more than try it, he was always sporting unusual and bright hairstyles throughout his playing career.
   But not sure this is something that lesser mortals would be able to get away with. I mean, if Chalkie were to walk in the pub with this haircut one night... well, he wouldn't do it again in a hurry I can tell you.

GERVINHO

Just the other day I was looking at Flo's mop thinking, 'what does that remind me of?' This style obviously has been influenced by that trusty household cleaning apparatus, and you wonder why has it not be in fashion before? Do I really have to answer that!
   My advice to Gervinho, chop it off and give it to Jack, he could probably make better use of it.

I NEVER HAVE TO USE MY MOP, ANDY IS USUALLY ON THE FLOOR, WITH A STRAW BEFORE I CAN EVEN GET IT OUT OF THE BUCKET!

112

BOBBY CHARLTON

Ah, Bobby. England's highest scoring player of all time and most of those goals from midfield. The lynchpin of the Manchester United and England teams for so long, a true national hero. However, for those who were not lucky enough to see him play, their most abiding memory of Bobby Charlton is that comb-over. Not so much a problem haircut as a problem with the lack of a hair cut. Still, he could play football could Bobby.

TONY DALEY

Ah the 90's, what a decade (I think...hic...). However for haircuts there were some that we can definitely forget, especially this creation which I suppose you would call the permed-mohican-that-gets-in-your-eyes look. I suppose we can sort of forgive Mr Daley for this look, after he produced one of the most memorable solo goals ever back in 1990 against Luton Town - although on the other hand, what was he thinking?!

KEVIN KEEGAN

I'd love it, love it if Kevin Keegan still had this haircut today, though I doubt anyone else would. Footballer's hairstyles started to go really wrong in the seventies and Keegan was as guilty as anyone else at the time - although to be fair, finding a footballer who actually had a decent mop in the decade of disco is probably an impossible task.

It's not so much that tastes have changed, just that good taste took a long well earned holiday for a while...

RIO FERDINAND

Cockney's are famed for their cheeky sense of humour, so when Rio Ferdinand was banned for eight months back in 2003 supporters of his former club West Ham came up with the chant "His name is Rio and he watches from the stand" to the tune of the Duran Duran hit Rio. Classic. Sadly Rio didn't spend that time off working on the perfect haircut. In fact, not that long afterwards he was seen sporting this cornrow effort. Now, the cornrow works best with mean and moody types, but no matter how hard our Rio tries he's just a bit too nice to pull it off. Less Snoop Dogg, more Snoopy.

CHRIS WADDLE

Ah, the mullet. Probably, in my humble opinion, the worst hair-style to ever grace a football pitch. If Becks couldn't make the mullet work, poor old Chris Waddle didn't stand a chance. There's nothing good about a mullet, you can't style it off as retro or old school. It just looks naff. Chalkie tried to grow one once and even his dog wouldn't be seen out with him in public.

Everybody usually remembers where they were when major events occurred but, for some reason, Andy's memory is a bit hazy!! So, to remind him, here are a few classic Andy strips from some famous dates in history...

GOOD FRIDAY PEACE AGREEMENT
Issue: 11 April, 1998

UK DECIMALISATION STARTS
Issue: 15 February, 1971

WHERE WERE YOU?

THE WORD OF CAFF

WORD SEARCH

A	S	U	B	S	T	I	T	U	T	E	F	H
T	D	I	S	S	E	N	T	T	H	T	U	E
T	F	O	O	T	B	A	L	L	R	A	L	A
A	R	C	S	B	O	O	T	S	O	C	L	D
C	D	O	C	D	U	M	M	Y	W	K	B	E
K	O	R	O	O	U	X	B	N	I	L	A	R
E	X	N	R	F	P	L	O	R	N	E	C	H
R	W	E	E	G	O	I	W	E	H	Z	K	G
L	I	R	C	N	T	U	T	D	H	S	I	L
C	N	K	O	U	P	H	L	C	S	D	G	O
H	G	I	A	T	H	K	N	A	H	I	O	V
I	E	C	C	Q	Y	E	P	R	O	V	A	E
P	R	K	H	S	B	J	O	D	T	E	L	S

Football, Football, Football. We love it, but can you tackle the puzzle and find all the words below?

ATTACKER	DIVE	PITCH
BENCH	DUMMY	RED CARD
BOOTS	FOOTBALL	SCORE
CAUTION	FOUL	SHOT
CHIP	FULL BACK	SUBSTITUTE
COACH	GLOVES	TACKLE
CORNER KICK	GOAL	THROW-IN
CROSS	HEADER	WINGER
DISSENT	PASS	

OCTOBER

THURSDAY

1

FRIDAY

2

SATURDAY

3

SUNDAY

4

MONDAY

5

TUESDAY

6

WEDNESDAY

7

THURSDAY

8

FRIDAY

9

SATURDAY

10

SUNDAY

11

MONDAY

12

TUESDAY

13

WEDNESDAY

14

THURSDAY

15

FRIDAY

16

THINGS TO DO

SATURDAY

17

SUNDAY

18

MONDAY

19

TUESDAY

20

WEDNESDAY

21

THURSDAY

22

FRIDAY

23

SATURDAY

24

SUNDAY

25

MONDAY

26

TUESDAY

27

WEDNESDAY

28

THURSDAY

29

FRIDAY

30

SATURDAY

31

THINGS TO DO

SPORTING EVENTS TO KEEP AN EYE OUT FOR
Football – 2015 FIFA U–17 World Cup – 17th October to 8th November
Horse Racing – Prix de L'Arc de Triomphe 2015
Cricket – England tour of Pakistan

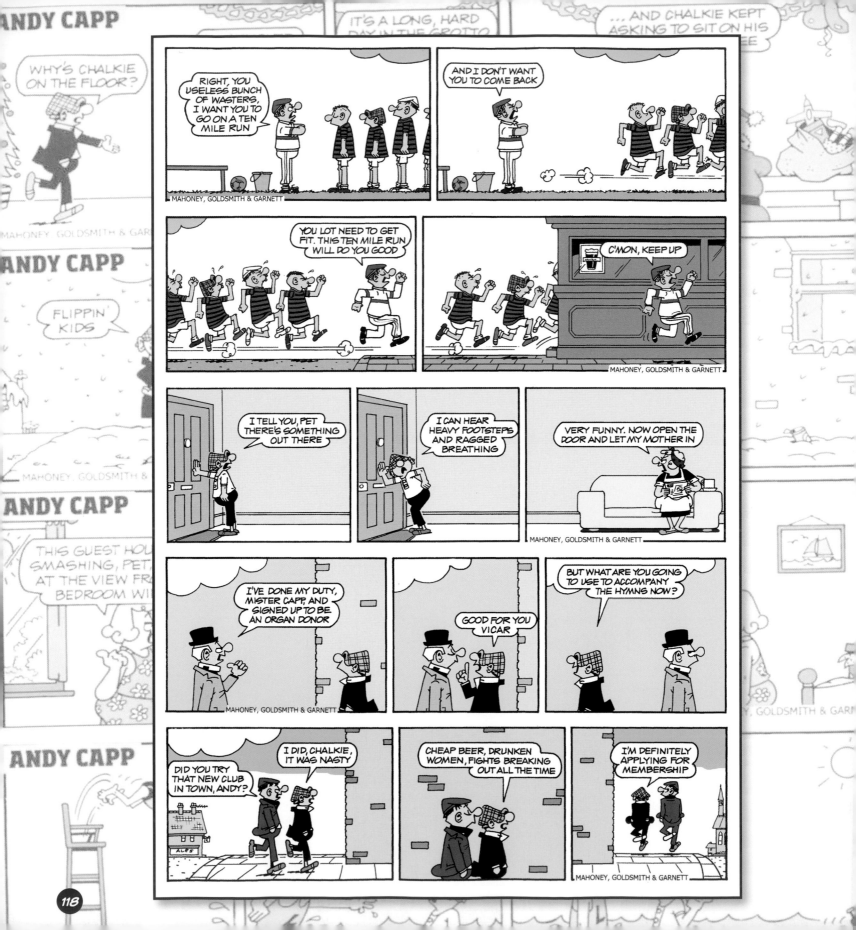

ASK ANDY

GOT A PROBLEM?
CONSIDER IT SOLVED!

Dear Andy,
You seem to fall in the canal a lot on your way back from the pub. Could you not take another route home to avoid any more soakings?

Kath, Kendal.

ANDY'S REPLY

Hi Kath, yes, tell me about it. I've spent more time in that blinkin' canal than I care to remember.

Once I've had a beer, or three, I seem to operate on auto pilot and go home the same way I came. Also, it's very dark at that time of night in my town and some of those narrow streets can get very confusing – who knows where I might end up? One other reason is, there's quite a few pubs I'd pass if I took other routes and I owe most people money in them so I'd rather not risk bumping into anyone like that.

Dear Andy,
My girlfriend recently dumped me because she said I spend too much time in the pub with my mates, or going to football when I should be taking her out. What can I do to get her back?

Nathan, Worksop.

ANDY'S REPLY

This is an easy one, Nathan. Your mates and football are clearly important to you, just like any normal bloke. And you are obviously fond of this lass. So, why not combine the two? Tell her you'll take her out more but go to the pub. You don't have to stand with yer pals, but every time ye get up to go to the bar, ye'll be able to have a natter with them before popping back with the drinks. And if she fancies a change, why not take her to the football? What could possibly go wrong?

Dear Andy,
One of my mates down the pub is turning into a real bore since he got a new girlfriend. He's started talking about the economy, films and the theatre instead of the usual football, birds, beer and cars. Is there anything we can do to snap him out of it?

Frank, Chester-le-Street.

ANDY'S REPLY

Sounds terrible, Frankie lad, but it would appear yer old pal is in love. He's clearly not himself. This often happens to fellas when they meet a new lass. No doubt she's nagged him silly about how boring it is just going down the pub with yer mates all the time, like, and decided he needs a bit of "culture." She's probably whisked him off to art galleries and to see fancy films and the like. My only advice is to leave the lad to it for a while. Mark my words, after putting up with all that nonsense for a few weeks, he'll be gagging to get back to nattering about beer, pigeons and football.

Dear Andy,
I always appear to be skint. Mind you, I don't work cos I can't be bothered. Could you give me some tips on how to make my meagre dole money go further?

Don, Sheffield.

ANDY'S REPLY

Don, Don, Don... My first piece of advice is never admit you can't be bothered to work. Always make it look like you're interested in jobs then think of an excuse why you can't do them. I've come up with some crackers in my time, but that's another story. As for yer cash, well, ye have t'surround yersel with decent pals who have a plentiful supply. With a bit of charm and humour they'll be longing for yer company and won't mind standing ye drinks all night, like.

120

ANDY'S GUIDE TO RUGBY

The rugby world cup is fast approaching and I don't know about you, but I love the sight of all those massive blokes crashing into each other while chasing an egg-shaped ball and trying to put the flamin' thing behind a line while others are seemingly trying to kill 'em. There's nowt better than being allowed to clump folk without PC Braithwaite carting me off down the nick. Here's a few pointers for those of you that haven't a clue what's going on in rugby...

WHICH ONE? Rugby Union is the posh one and Rugby League is the one working class lads like me traditionally play. Some bloke in the pub told me there used to be just one type of rugby but a load of fellas in the north started getting compensated for missing work to play which the southerners didn't like so they formed a breakaway mob. At least, I think that's what he said, he'd just bought me a beer and I kinda switched off a bit.

SCRUMS This is where blokes bend down and crash into each other while another player throws the ball in so one of them can grab hold of it and pass it to a team-mate. I never get involved with scrums myself just in case it collapses and I end up with all those massive 20st fellas on top of me.

> HE TRIED EXPLAINING THIS TO ME ONCE AND LOST HIS TEMPER WHEN I ASKED WHY THE GOAL IS SHAPED LIKE AN 'H' AND DOESN'T HAVE A NET.

SCORING In League a try is worth four points, a goal two and a drop goal one. Whereas in Union, puff pant, a try gives you five points, a conversion (kicking the ball over the middle of the 'H' shaped posts) is worth two and a penalty or drop goal, three.

DIFFERENCES League has 13 players, Union has 15, which sounds like hard work to me. In League you have have t'give the ball away after six tackles without scoring, that's what Big Dave said anyway. But in the other one ye don't. Are ye keeping up with me?

CROWD Unlike football supporters, rugby fans tend to be a lot more polite and gracious, as do the players. Instead of calling the ref all the names under the flamin' sun, with a few swearwords thrown in for good measure, they seem to just accept his decision, which is a bit blinkin' weird.

> NO. HAVE YOU BEEN ON THE BEER?

> ANDY TENDS TO FORGET THIS WHEN HE'S PLAYING. JUST LAST WEEK HE CHASED THE REF AROUND THE PITCH AND RUGBY TACKLED HIM COS HE GAVE A PENALTY AGAINST HIM. OH, AND HE CALLED HIM EVERY NAME UNDER THE SUN.

DRINKING Rugby and booze go hand in hand. I mean, after knocking lumps out of each other for 80 minutes these fellas deserve a pint, or seven, to relax and mull over the match. It also helps numb all that pain. Alright, some of those drinking games can go a bit far and often blokes end up naked and hanging from street signs, which Flo and Ruby don't see anything wrong with, but on the whole it's all good natured fun.

FIGHTS In rugby it seems OK for blokes to have a massive scrap. The ref just looks on as they knock seven bells out of each other then blows his whistle in an angry fashion and everyone stops. The only reason they have physios in this game is to bring bandages and plasters on to patch up the players before they carry on with the match.

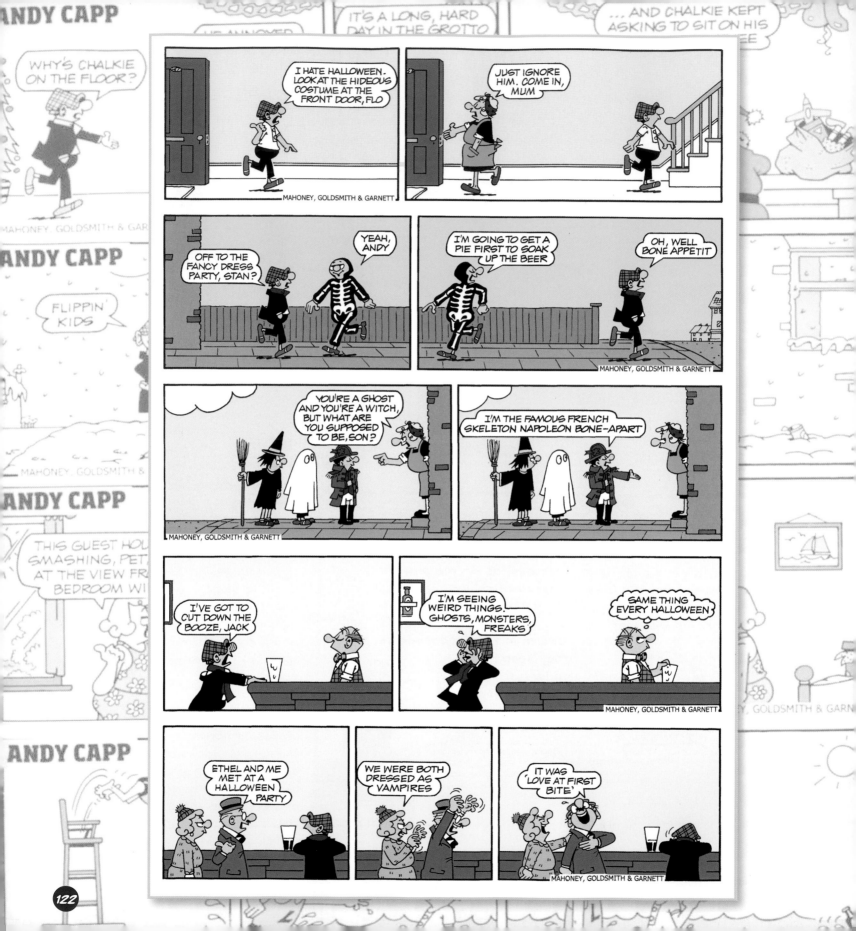

CHALKIE'S CHUCKLES

Two cannibals eating a clown.
One says to the other: "Does this taste funny to you?"

A woman goes to the local paper's office to see that the obituary for her recently deceased husband is published. The obit editor informs her that there is a charge of 50 pence per word. She pauses, reflects, and then says: "Well then, let it read: 'Evan Davis died'."

Amused at the woman's thrift, the editor tells her that there is a seven-word minimum for all obituaries. She thinks it over and in a few seconds says, "In that case, let it read, – 'Evan Davis died, golf clubs for sale'."

I went to the doctor. He said: "You've got a very serious illness."
I replied: "I want a second opinion."
He said: "All right, you're ugly as well."

Two friends sitting down having a pint together. The first man says: "I've been feeling so ill recently, I've thought about killing myself.'"
"Oh no, that's terrible," the second man responds.'
"Then, yesterday, I actually went to do it... I was gonna take 100 painkillers."
"Well, what happened?'"
"'I took one and felt a whole lot better."

A pregnant woman gets into a car accident and falls into a deep coma. Asleep for nearly six months, she wakes up and sees that she is no longer pregnant. Frantically, she asks the doctor about her baby. The doctor replies, "Ma'am, you had twins! A boy and a girl. The babies are fine. Your brother came in and named them."

The woman thinks to herself, "Oh no, not my brother – he's an idiot!" Expecting the worst, she asks the doctor, "Well, what's the girl's name?" "Denise," the doctor says. The new mother thinks, "Wow, that's not a bad name! Guess I was wrong about my brother. I like Denise!" Then she asks the doctor, "What's the boy's name?" The doctor replies, "DeNephew."

A man walks into a flower shop and says, "I need some flowers."
"Of course," the florist says. "What do you have in mind?"
"I'm not really sure."
The florist says, "Let me ask that a different way. What exactly have you done?"

Why did the scarecrow win a nobel prize?

He was outstanding in his field

GHOUL TORMENTS NORTHERN TOWN?

Mirror
INVESTIGATES

By Paul T Geist, Mirror
Paranormal Investigator

A mysterious ghoul stalking the streets at night? Objects moving of their own accord? Unearthly noises that chill all who hear them to the bone? For most of us, spooky goings on are the stuff of fanciful ghost stories, but for the residents of one northern town those stories seem to have become all too real. We sent our top Mirror Paranormal Investigator to investigate what was really going on...

Hartlepool. A proud town with a fine history. The sort of place where the cheery residents still stop and talk together in the street, where even strangers nod and smile as they pass each other by.

But recent inexplicable events have cast a dark shadow over this once happy place and have caused some to wonder if that fine history isn't coming back to haunt this seaside haven.

The story begins only a few months ago, when a new job meant relocation to the town for a young couple, Paul and Sally Crabtree from London.

What should have been a new start for our young couple has turned into a waking nightmare.

For Paul and Sally their horrific ordeal began late last October, on the scariest night of the year. Halloween.

"It was late, and I'd only just got under the duvet myself when all of a sudden it happened! The sound of someone, something, shuffling and stumbling along the street outside, followed by a terrible and horrifying noise." I gently press Paul to continue. "It was like a banshee wail! Harrowing it was, a tortured soul crying out for mercy." Intrigued, I asked if the couple had actually seen anything? "Truth be told, I wasn't too keen on getting out of bed to look, but Sally insisted. Couldn't see nothing, though – street was covered in fog. But I could make out a few words, amidst all the screeching." I sat bolt upright, this was a key development. "What words?" I asked. "Whatever it was, it was desperate, begging someone... Just the same line, over and over – 'Please release me, let me go'."

I left Paul and Sally's shaking with excitement. What had they encountered? My investigations had to continue and so here it was that I met Charlie and Norville, two first time visitors to a local pub who had encountered this spectre for themselves.

I order a round of drinks and ask them for their story. Norville is strangely uneasy and completely preoccupied just sits staring at his glass. Charlie takes up my offer: "Well it were a right strange affair. We're not regulars here, much prefer the Slaughtered Lamb up on the moors above town but it were quiz night and we're not really ones for a quiz, are we Norville?" Norville doesn't respond, just continues his unbroken watch on his pint. "Anyway, so we thought we'd head into town for a change and ended up in here. Nice place, or so we thought." I raise an eyebrow, clearly we're about to cut to the chase. "Well, here we were, sitting at the bar, minding our own business like, when just like that it happens." I cut in, "What happens?" "Well, our drinks just disappear into thin air! As if by magic, one minute there they are and then the next - gone!" Drinks do not usually just disappear, I suggest that perhaps our two visitors having had a few already had simply lost count. "No chance, it were our first pint! We were proper looking forward to that ale!" A sob from Norville, but his vigilant watch continues. "It were just like that film" Charlie continues "Para-abnormal Activities or something."

I wonder if the staff knows anymore, surely they must have seen plenty of ghostly evidence? I ask Jack, the barman: "Jack, these gentlemen are clearly shaken by their experience in here, what can you tell me of these mysteriously vanishing drinks?" Jack chuckles, "Sounds like they had a visit from Andy." I gasp and ask incredulously: "The evil fiend has a name?" "Oh yes, Andy. I wouldn't say evil, more pesky to be honest. He's been hanging around in here for years, we've all learnt to love him as he's part of the furniture, but you have to tolerate the odd missing drink - Andy hates to see a pint glass without company. Don't worry lads, these beers are on me for your trouble like." I ask if any other strange activity has been recorded: "Well, he has been know to throw things, though mainly only at Guitar Bob during one of his sets on a Saturday night."

So there we are. I leave the pub as my time here has run out but we still have no answers, just more questions. The good folk of Hartlepool will continue to put up with their resident ghoul, the one they know as Andy. While I can only wonder at their hardy resilience.

But as you go about your daily lives I can only ask you to spare a thought for their suffering at the hands of this fiend. Poor souls.

GOODNIGHT, AND WHEREVER YOU ARE, SLEEP TIGHT.

LOOK BACK WITH ANDY

Everybody usually remembers where they were when major events occurred but, for some reason, Andy's memory is a bit hazy!! So, to remind him, here are a few classic Andy strips from some famous dates in history...

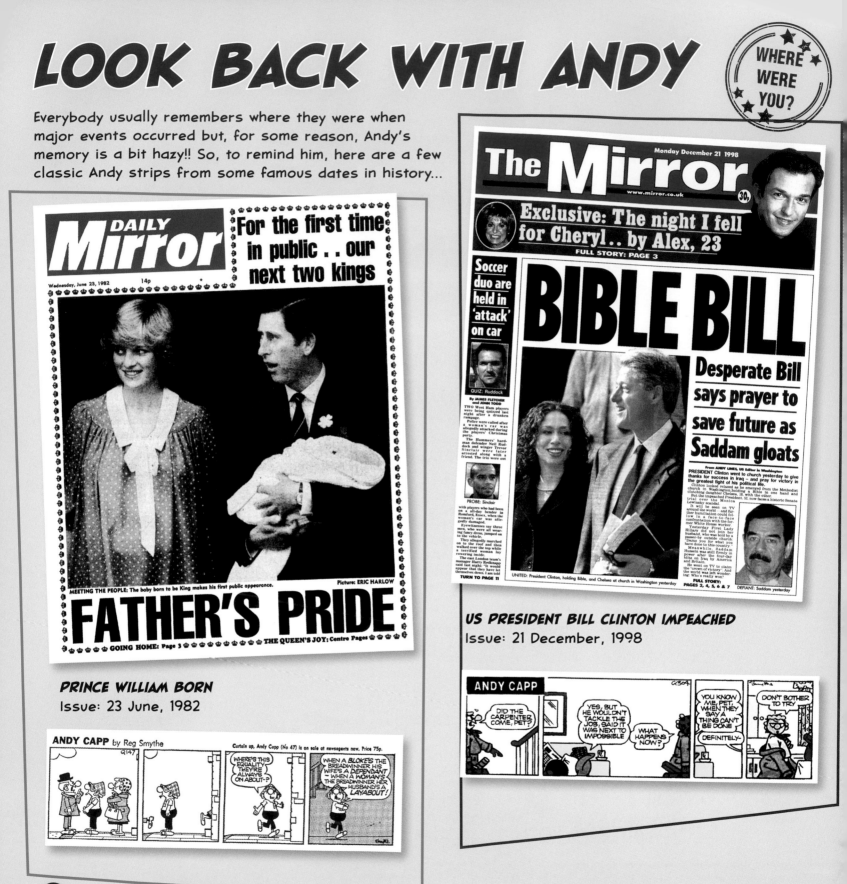

PRINCE WILLIAM BORN
Issue: 23 June, 1982

US PRESIDENT BILL CLINTON IMPEACHED
Issue: 21 December, 1998

126

JACK'S PUB QUIZ

TRANSPORT

1. Which iconic car was designed by Alec Issigonis in 1959?

2. Which famous motorcycle manufacturer was founded in Milwaukee, USA in 1903?

3. Which is Europe's busiest international airport: Heathrow or Frankfurt?

4. What name is given to a bicycle 'made for two'?

5. Boxster and Cayman are models of which sought-after motor?

6. What is the name of the double-decker bus designed for use by London Transport?

7. HMS Dreadnought was Britain's first nuclear-powered what?

8. Which two portly TV chefs used to travel about on their motor bike and sidecar?

9. Which manufacturer made the three-wheeled car 'the Robin', made famous in Only Fools and Horses?

10. In which year did Concorde make its first commercial flight: 1966 or 1976?

11. What in the history of transport was 'The Mallard'?

12. In which motor sport was Barry Sheene a World Champion in the 1970s?

NOVEMBER

SUNDAY

1

MONDAY

2

TUESDAY

3

WEDNESDAY

4

THURSDAY

5

FRIDAY

6

SATURDAY

7

SUNDAY

8

MONDAY

9

TUESDAY

10

WEDNESDAY

11

THURSDAY

12

FRIDAY

13

SATURDAY

14

SUNDAY

15

MONDAY

16

THINGS TO DO

TUESDAY

17

WEDNESDAY

18

THURSDAY

19

FRIDAY

20

SATURDAY

21

SUNDAY

22

MONDAY

23

TUESDAY

24

WEDNESDAY

25

THURSDAY

26

FRIDAY

27

SATURDAY

28

SUNDAY

29

MONDAY

30

St Andrew's Day (Scotland)

SPORTING EVENTS TO KEEP AN EYE OUT FOR
Horse Racing – Melbourne Cup – 3rd November
Tennis – Davis Cup Final
Tennis – ATP World Tour Finals
Rugby Union – Autumn Internationals

THINGS
TO DO

ROLL OUT THE BARREL

ANOTHER OF ANDY'S SCHEMES GOES PEAR – OR, RATHER, BARREL-SHAPED. CAN YOU SPOT 10 DIFFERENCES BETWEEN THE PICTURES?

ANDY'S GUIDE TO PUB ETIQUETTE

You've probably noticed I spend a fair bit of time in the boozer. Some folk think we locals just arrive and prop up the bar – which may be true to a certain extent, but the pub is also a very sociable place where friends are made, and often lost. Plus, there is a set of rules we abide by. For the first-time pub-goer, here's a list of dos and don'ts...

DO Put lots of good songs on the juke box. I love a great tune and I'd normally put them on myself but I'm usually short of change, or at least Flo is, so I can't.

> I'M USUALLY SHORT OF CHANGE COS I'VE HAD TO BUY HIM CRISPS, OR PEANUTS, OR SOMETHING AFTER HE'S MOANED THAT MY COOKING IS SO AWFUL HE'S STARVING.

DO Buy me a drink. I'm a veteran customer and I can tell you everything you need to know about pub etiquette. So stick with me and you won't go wrong.

> STICK WITH HIM MEANS DON'T GO OFF BUYING ANYONE ELSE DRINKS.

DO Let me buy drinks and put them on your tab. I will pay ye back, honest, and it stops those flippin' awkward moments when I get a round and Jack tells me I've reached the limit on my tab for the week.

> HE'S NORMALLY REACHED THE LIMIT ON HIS TAB FOR THE WEEK BY MONDAY, SO WHY ANYONE WOULD LET HIM IN ON THEIR TAB IS A MYSTERY.

DON'T Push in. There's nothing worse than someone at the bar trying to get served before someone else who's been waiting. It's the height of bad manners. If Chalkie has a tenner in his hand it's flamin' obvious he's getting him and me a drink, so wait your turn.

DON'T Listen to Chalkie. If he tells you anything bad about me he's just being bitter cos all the lasses chat to me and not him.

> ER, I'M JUST TELLING THEM THE TRUTH AND THE ONLY REASON LASSES CHAT TO HIM IS NORMALLY TO TELL HIM TO GET LOST AFTER HE'S BEEN PESTERING THEM FOR DRINKS.

DON'T Turn up after last orders expecting a drink from Jack, he's not one for bending the rules. Just last week I popped in on my way home from a darts night out at another pub. It was only one minute past 11, and he told me to sling me hook, despite the fact I was doing him a favour by bringing his blinking' darts back.

DO Tell Guitar Bob he's rubbish. I know he's not, but it makes me chuckle when he thinks he's playing really well and someone shouts out "gerroff" (usually me). I love watching his face crumple.

> I DON'T MIND HECKLERS BUT I DO GET A BIT MIFFED WITH ANDY CAPP ORDERING PEOPLE TO HECKLE ME JUST COS HIS HECKLING IS HAVING NO AFFECT ON ME.

CHALKIE'S CHUCKLES

Two brooms were hanging in the closet and after a while they got to know each other so well, they decided to get married.

One broom was, of course, the bride broom, the other the groom broom.

The bride broom looked very beautiful in her white dress. The groom broom was handsome and suave in his tuxedo. The wedding was lovely.

After the wedding, at the wedding dinner, the bride-broom leaned over and said to the groom-broom, "I think I am going to have a little dust broom!!!"

"IMPOSSIBLE!!" said the groom broom.

"WE HAVEN'T EVEN SWEPT TOGETHER!"

A man is at the doctors for some test results. The doctor looks at his notes.
Doc: "I'm afraid the results are very bad, Mr Brown - you've not very long to live at all."
Man: "How long, doc?"
Doc: "10..."
Man: "I only have 10 weeks to live?"
Doc: *shakes head* "...9"

I just got dumped by my girlfriend, who is a trampolinist.
She had terrible mood swings, always up and down and up and down.
My last girlfriend before that was in the Scottish Javelin squad – she chucked me, too.

Went to the butchers the other day and bet him £20 that he couldn't reach the meat on the top shelf He said: "Nah, steaks are too high"

What do you call an exploding monkey?
A Babboom.

What do you call cheese that isn't yours?
Nacho cheese!

Man goes into a doctors with a strawberry on his head.
Doctor says: "I got some cream you can put on that."

SONG	CAN YOU FILL IN THE MISSING WORDS?
1. **WATERLOO**	Couldn't _____ __ _ wanted to
2. **LIKE A VIRGIN**	Touched for the very _____ ____
3. **SUMMER NIGHTS**	He showed off _____ _____
4. **DELILAH**	__ _____ ____ come to break down the door
5. **HEY JUDE**	___'_ _____ ___ _____ upon your shoulders
6. **SWEET CAROLINE**	Will it fill up with _____ ___
7. **AMERICAN PIE**	Drove __ _____ to the levee, but the levee was dry
8. **BROWN EYED GIRL**	Skipping and _ _____
9. **BOHEMIAN RHAPSODY**	I'm just a poor boy, _ ____ __ _____
10. **DON'T STOP BELIEVIN'**	Some were born to ____ ___ _____
11. **LIVIN' ON A PRAYER**	____ __ ____ and we'll make it – I swear
12. **BEAT IT**	No one wants to be _____

GUITAR BOB'S

MISSING
LYRICS
QUIZ

SONG

13. **ROAR**　　　　　　　　I got the ___ __ ___ _____

14. **I WALK THE LINE**　　　I keep a _____ _____ on this heart of mine

15. **THE WONDER OF YOU**　You give me hope ___ _____

16. **PRICE TAG**　　　　　　We just wanna make ___ _____ _____

17. **EARTH SONG**　　　　　What about sunrise, ____ _____ ____

18. **BACK FOR GOOD**　　　Whatever I said, whatever I did, _ ____'_ ____ __

19. **ROTTERDAM**　　　　　This could be Rotterdam __ _____

20. **BERMUDA TRIANGLE**　Bermuda Triangle, it makes people _____

21. **UMBRELLA**　　　　　　When the sun shines, we'll _____ _____

22. **SPACE ODDITY**　　　　_____ _____ to Major Tom

23. **EBONY AND IVORY**　　Ebony and Ivory, live together in _____ _____

24. **VENUS**　　　　　　　I'm your Venus, I'm your fire, at ____ _____

25. **CARELESS WHISPER**　_____ ____ have got no rhythm

LOOK BACK WITH ANDY

Everybody usually remembers where they were when major events occurred but, for some reason, Andy's memory is a bit hazy!! So, to remind him, here are a few classic Andy strips from some famous dates in history...

MARGARET THATCHER RESIGNS AS PRIME MINISTER
Issue: 29 November, 1990

BRITISH CONCORDE MAIDEN FLIGHT
Issue: 10 April, 1969

WHERE WERE YOU?

THE WORD OF CAPP

```
B O O K M A K E R S T
J S Q W S T L E G E R
K T U B N Y V F R P I
S A R Q B E T O A A P
T K J R O J R D N D L
A E E I A J A D D E
R D G W K D I S S O C
T E M D S T N M T C R
F G U A E D E Q A K O
S T A L L S R M N J W
S T A B L E L A D M N
```

WORD SEARCH

Nags, Gee Gees, and whatever else you like to call the Sport of Kings. Can you find all the words in this horsey puzzle?

BOOKMAKERS	OWNER	STALLS
DERBY	PADDOCK	START
GRANDSTAND	ST LEGER	STUD
OAKS	STABLE LAD	TRAINER
ODDS	STAKE	TRIPLE CROWN

DECEMBER

TUESDAY

1

WEDNESDAY

2

THURSDAY

3

FRIDAY

4

SATURDAY

5

SUNDAY

6

MONDAY

7

TUESDAY

8

WEDNESDAY

9

THURSDAY

10

FRIDAY

11

SATURDAY

12

SUNDAY

13

MONDAY

14

TUESDAY

15

WEDNESDAY

16

THINGS TO DO

THURSDAY

17

FRIDAY

18

SATURDAY

19

SUNDAY

20

MONDAY

21

TUESDAY

22

WEDNESDAY

23

THURSDAY

24

FRIDAY

25

Christmas Day

SATURDAY

26

Boxing Day

SUNDAY

27

MONDAY

28

Bank Holiday

TUESDAY

29

WEDNESDAY

30

THURSDAY

31

SPORTING EVENTS TO KEEP AN EYE OUT FOR
Cricket – England tour of South Africa
Football – 2015 FIFA Club World Cup
Darts – World Darts Championship
Snooker – UK Championship

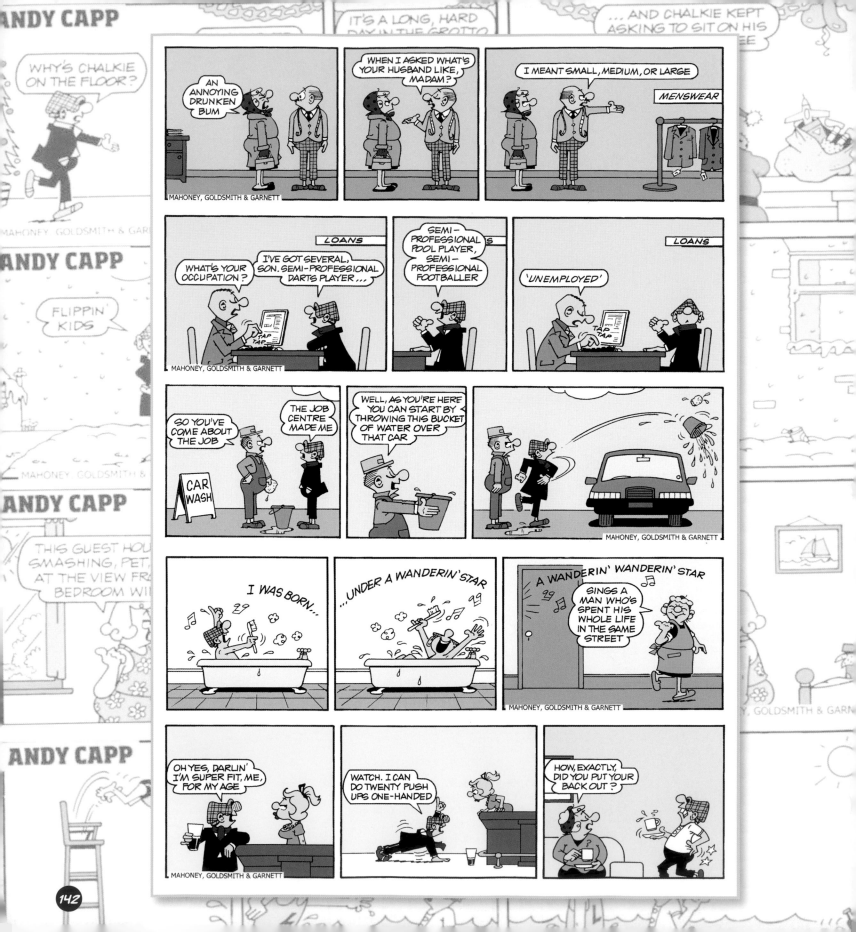

THE VICAR'S CHRISTMAS MESSAGE

HELLO TO YOU ALL AND MERRY CHRISTMAS.

This is an exciting time for everyone, with children looking forward to their presents as parents prepare to experience the warm glow of joy that comes from seeing those happy little faces. As well as, of course, all the others who exchange gifts.

But while you're all having fun, be it at home or at the office party, I want you to remember the true significance of this festive period - that God sent his only son, Jesus, to take away the sins of the world.

I know this is a time of giving, when we should be reaching out to the needy amongst us, but that does not mean I can hand out cash from church collections to a certain individual just so they can go out with mates and have a few drinks (I think you have a good idea who that individual I'm referring to is).

And while we are on the subject of the needy, the food left at the back of the church from many of the kind souls in our congregation is meant for the less well off in our community - not for people on their way home from a night out boozing who fancy a quick snack because they're too late for the chip shop (mentioning no names, but the initials 'AC' may give you a clue).

When Jesus was born, he was brought gifts of gold, frankincense and myrrh and we carry on that symbol of giving with our exchange of presents today. But do not be weighed down by the burden of material expectancies. Be grateful for what you have in your loving family and friends. As Andy Capp once said to me: "What would I do without my Flo, Vicar?" Although I was later told by his friend Chalkie, in what I thought was rather a disappointing admission, he meant what would he do without Flo's purse.

So, enjoy the festivities and I hope to see you all at the various services throughout this time, put on to celebrate the birth of our Lord. Although I'd like to remind those of you with a fondness for the pub that the midnight service on Christmas Eve is not there just for somewhere to have a lie down at the back after you've been thrown out of the bar. You know who you are - and your drunken attempts at changing the words, 'While Shepherds Watched Their Flocks by Night' to 'While Shepherds Washed Their Locks...' last year was not as funny as you clearly found it.

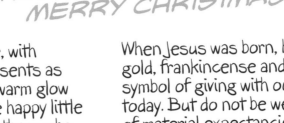

ANDY'S GUIDE TO CHRISTMAS

Flamin' 'ell, where did that year go? It seems like only yesterday that I was giving you all tips on how to shake off the yuletide excess and yet here I am preparing for another busy festive period. It's a great time, though, isn't it? Flo's purse is bursting with her Christmas bonus and Jack's promised us a free mince pie each – although he's adamant he won't swap it for a pint, which I think is a bit mean given that it's a time of giving. Anyway, Merry Christmas and Happy New Year to you all. I hope my tips and pages of fun have helped you have a laughter-filled year. My final words of advice are on how to enjoy the festivities...

TURKEY AND TRIMMINGS What can beat a Christmas dinner? We have ours down at the pub these days. I told Flo it would take the pressure off her as I know how stressful it can be cooking such a meal but, between you and me, I prefer Jack's cooking.

MISTLETOE There's always a bit of this hanging over the bar and the best bet is to stand right by it so you get a peck or two from any lasses that come in. I do this every year but I think Jack may have put it in a place where it's not easily seen cos all the girls seem to gather at the other end of the counter. I can only assume they haven't noticed it.

> THEY'VE SEEN IT ALRIGHT BUT THEY'RE WORRIED THEY MIGHT HAVE TO BUY HIM A DRINK IF THEY GO OVER. THEY'RE NOT DAFT.

> I HAVE TO ADMIT, MR CAPP IS AT THIS SERVICE YEAR IN, YEAR OUT, WITHOUT FAIL. BUT I'M A LITTLE DISAPPOINTED AT HIS SNORING. IT CAN BE QUITE DISCONCERTING FOR OTHER MEMBERS OF THE CONGREGATION WHEN HE FALLS OFF THE PEW HE'S LYING ON DURING THE QUIET PRAYER MOMENTS.

MIDNIGHT CHURCH SERVICE The vicar always encourages us to attend this and I'm happy to oblige, especially as the building has heating and is on the way home from the pub.

OFFICE PARTIES I know I don't work in an office (yes, alright, Flo, I don't work at all – there's no need to remind everyone) but when they are having their bashes in my local pub I join in just to be sociable because it would be rude not to. And being a time of giving, I often ask them to give me a pint or two.

> THEY USUALLY CAVE IN TO HIS REQUESTS, JUST TO GET RID OF HIM, WHILE WISHING HIM A MERRY CHRISTMAS, OF COURSE.

> PERHAPS IT'S DYING OUT BECAUSE CERTAIN PEOPLE KEEP YELLING AT THEM TO KEEP THE NOISE DOWN WHILE THEY'RE TRYING TO WATCH THE TELLY AND GUZZLE ALE. MENTIONING NO NAMES, LIKE.

CAROLS There's nothing better than the sound of festive songs at your doorstep while yer sipping a beer in front of a nice warm fire. Sadly, this is a tradition that seems to be dying out in Britain, so come on boys and girls, get back out there and keep us entertained.

BOXING DAY SALES This is where Flo and Ruby come into their own. I've never seen such a determined pair trying to get to the front of the queue for the bargains. Last year they nearly knocked the security guard at the department store unconscious when he opened the door, after trampling half of the other women who were in front of them.

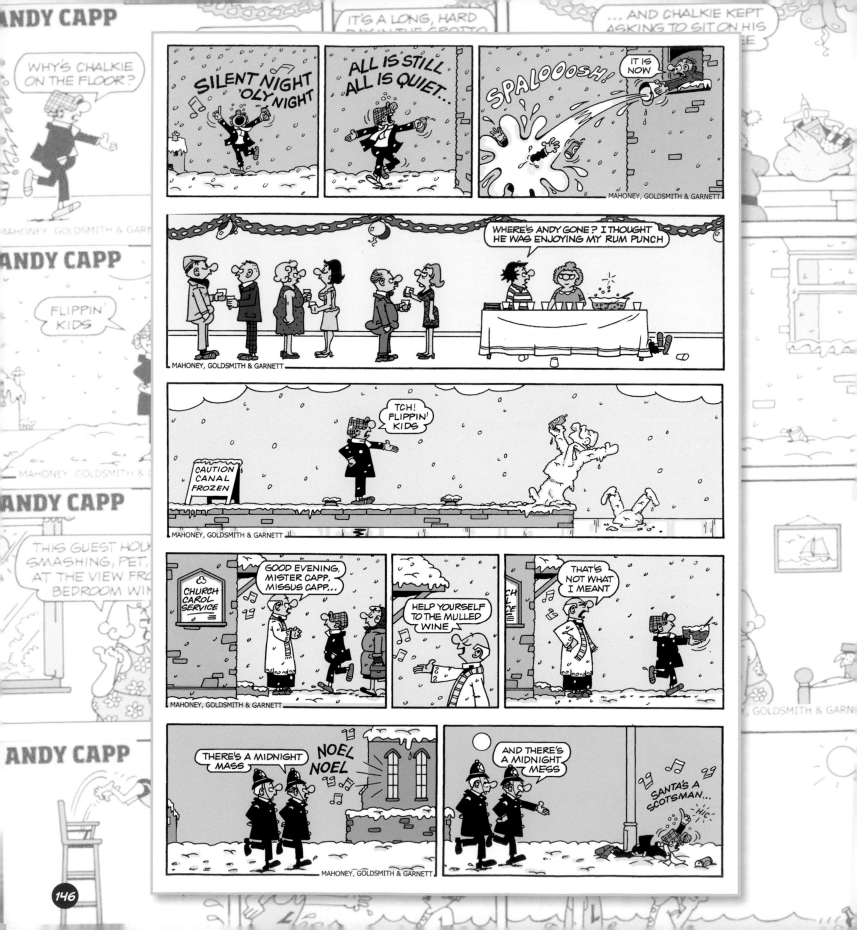

CHALKIE'S CHUCKLES

What's green and runs around the house? A hedge.

Three men died on Christmas Eve, and were met by Saint Peter at the pearly gates.

"In honour of this holy season," Saint Peter said. "You must each possess something that symbolises Christmas to get into Heaven."

The first man fumbled through his pockets and pulled out a lighter. He flicked it on. "It represents a candle," he said

"You may pass through the pearly gates," Saint Peter said.

The second man reached into his pocket and pulled out a set of keys.

He shook them and said, "They're bells."

Saint Peter said, "You may pass through the pearly gates."

The third man started searching desperately through his pockets and finally pulled out a pair of women's panties.

Saint Peter looked at the man with a raised eyebrow and asked, "And just what do these symbolise?"

The man replied, "These are Carol's."

The family gathered at the grandparents' home for their Christmas dinner.

Everyone was seated around the table.

The food arrived and little Johnny started eating immediately.

"Johnny, please wait until we say grace," said his mother.

"I don't need to," said Johnny.

"Of course you do," his mother insisted. "We always say a prayer before eating at our house."

"That's at our house," said Johnny. "This is Grandma's house and she knows how to cook."

Why are skeletons always so calm?

Because it's very difficult to get under their skin.

A man has been found guilty of overusing commas. The judge warned him to expect a very long sentence.

I went to a fancy dress party last night covered in gooseberries and cream.

I looked like a right fool.

A man walks into a bookshop and says "I hope you don't have a book on reverse psychology."

GIVE IT A REST, ANDY.

HA HA, LAST YEAR OUR TURKEY WAS SO BURNT I COULDN'T TELL THE DIFFERENCE BETWEEN IT AND THE CHRISTMAS PUD.

FLO'S KITCHEN

Hello again everyone and Merry Christmas. I was going to do a traditional turkey with all the trimmings recipe for you, but you probably all know how to do that already. So, I thought I'd share how to make a delicious Christmas pud with you instead. After all, no yuletide roast would be complete without one.

Right, folks, here's a list of what you'll need before embarking on this tasty adventure. This will serve up to eight people, so you can have loads of seconds if you want – just to be sociable, you understand. It also takes ages, so I'd start doing it a good week or more before Christmas Day.

INGREDIENTS

450g dried mixed fruit including raisins or currants
25g mixed candied peel, chopped up finely
One cooking apple, peeled, cored and chopped
Grated zest and juice
1/2 large orange and 1/2 lemon
4 tbsp brandy. You'll need a little extra for pouring over the pudding at end
55 g self-raising flour
1 level tsp ground mixed spice
1-1/2 tsp ground cinnamon
110 g shredded suet
110g brown sugar
110 g white bread crumbs
25 g almonds, chopped
2 big eggs

METHOD:

1) Lightly butter a 1.4 litre pudding basin.

2) Place the dried fruits, candied peel, apple, orange and lemon juice into a large mixing bowl. Add the brandy and stir. Cover bowl with a tea towel and leave to marinate for a couple of hours. Or even better, overnight.

3) Stir together the flour, spice and cinnamon in a large mixing bowl. Add suet, sugar, zest, breadcrumbs, nuts and stir until well mixed. Add the marinated dried fruits and stir again.

4) Beat the eggs in a small bowl then stir into the dry ingredients. Mix should be soft.

5) Spoon mixture into the greased pudding basin, pressing it down with spoon. Cover with two layers of greaseproof paper, then a layer of aluminium foil. Tie with string.

 Flamin' 'eck, what a palaver. So this is what you get up to when me 'n' Chalkie are down the pub in the nights before Christmas?

 I'm beginning to wonder if it's worth it. Anyway, carrying on...

6) Place pudding in a steamer over a big pan of simmering water and steam for seven hours. Check water level frequently so it never boils dry. The pudding should be deep brown when cooked.

7) Remove from the steamer and cool. Take off the paper, prick pudding with a spike or skewer and pour in a little brandy. Cover with fresh greaseproof paper and tie up again with string. Store in a cool dry place until Christmas day. Don't be tempted to eat it immediately (I know, I have been in the past) after cooking as it will collapse. Flavours also need time to mature. If you do succumb, don't worry too much, you've got plenty of time to make another heh heh.

On Christmas day, reheat the pudding by steaming again for an hour. Serve with brandy, brandy butter, cognac or custard.

DID SOMEONE MENTION BRANDY? NOW WE'RE TALKING. CAN I HELP, PET?

NO, SHOVE OFF. ANYWAY, FOLKS, AS A FINAL AND VERY YULETIDE TOUCH, WARM THE BRANDY OR COGNAC IN A PAN, POUR OVER THE PUDDING AND SET LIGHT TO IT.

DON'T YOU THINK YOU'VE BURNT ENOUGH THINGS WITHOUT SETTING THE FLAMIN' PUDDING ON FIRE?

I CAN SEE THIS IS GOING TO BE ONE OF THOSE CHRISTMAS DAYS WITH HIM IN THIS SORT OF MOOD. MAYBE IT'S BECAUSE MY MOTHER IS COMING ROUND. ANYWAY, HAPPY CHRISTMAS TO YOU ALL AND ENJOY YOUR PUDDING.

LOOK BACK WITH ANDY

Everybody usually remembers where they were when major events occurred but, for some reason, Andy's memory is a bit hazy!! So, to remind him, here are a few classic Andy strips from some famous dates in history...

MILLENNIUM
Issue: 1 January, 2000

BERLIN WALL FALLS
Issue: 10 November, 1989

PRINCE HARRY BORN
Issue: 17 August, 1984

ENGLAND GET TO THE 1966 WORLD CUP FINAL
Issue: 27 July, 1966

WHERE WERE YOU?

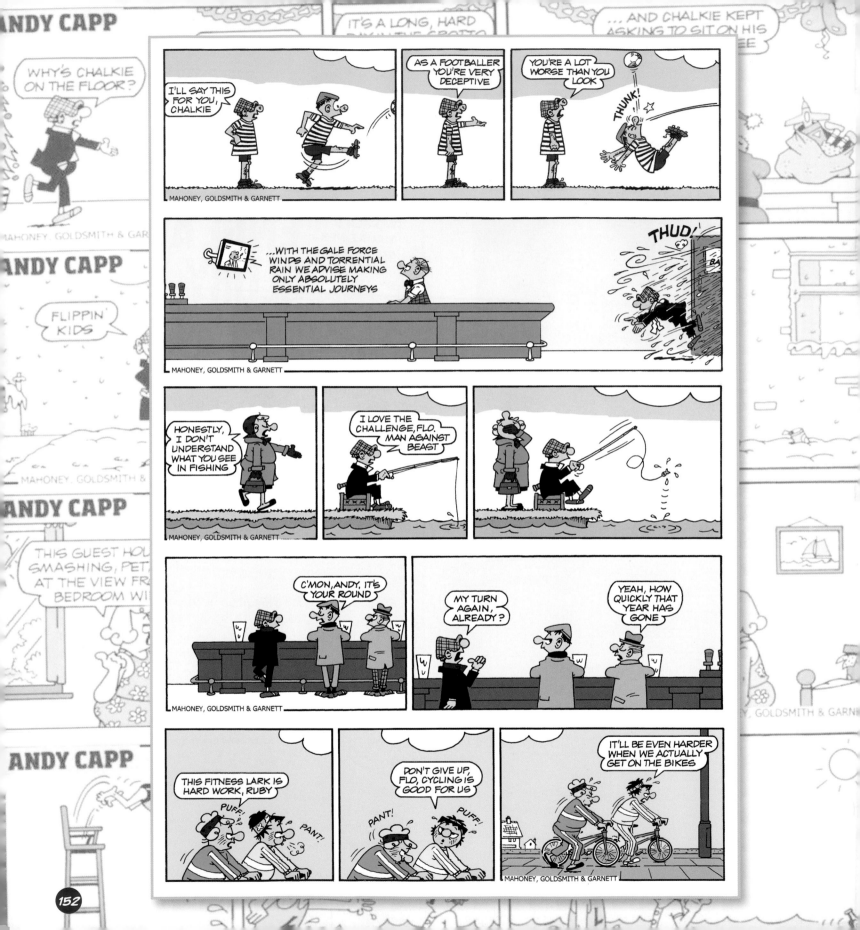

JACK'S FESTIVE BUMPER PUB QUIZ

1. Which bird of the crow family shares its name with a chess piece?

2. Who was the drummer with The Beatles?

3. Prior to decimalisation in the UK, what term was given to a coin worth two shillings?

4. The 'O' on a roulette wheel is usually which colour?

5. What was the alter ego of Steve Austin, a character played by Lee Majors in a 70's TV series?

6. Who succeeded Tony Blair as Prime Minister of Great Britain?

7. What do Chessington, Thorpe Park and Alton Towers have in common?

8. Sherwood Forest is associated with which historical outlaw?

9. What nationality is golfer, Padraig Harrington?

10. Which car manufacturer has in the past produced models called the Cortina, Capri and Consul?

11. The cities of Dundee and Perth stand on which Scottish river?

12. Which number sits between 3 and 7 on a dartboard?

13. Which Kent town is Europe's busiest ferry port?

14. In horseracing, which race is the fillies' equivalent of the Derby?

15. Who is the main presenter of the TV show 'Top Gear'?

16. In which TV quiz show did contestants say, "I'll have a 'P' please, Bob"?

17. One of Andy's favourite pints is IPA – what do the initials stand for?

18. What nationality is four-time World Snooker Champion, John Higgins?

19. Casino Royale was the first novel by which writer?

20. In which English seaside resort is the 'Golden Mile'?

21. A Penny Farthing was an old type of which mode of transport?

22. Which alloy of tin and lead is used to make beer tankards?

23. Which type of beer is marketed as 'Probably the best beer in the world'?

24. How many colours are there on a Rubik's Cube?

25. Whose hit records include 'Poker Face' and 'Bad Romance'?

SOLUTIONS

Opening Time Disaster

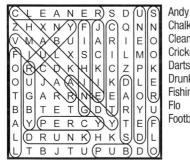

THE WORD OF CAPP

Andy
Chalkie
Cleaner
Cricket
Darts
Drunk
Fishing
Flo
Football

Jackie
Percy
Pub
Ruby
Rugby
Snooker
Unemployed
Vicar

Jack's Pub Quiz – Television

1. Hale and Pace
2. Dot Cotton (or Dot Branning)
3. Victor Meldrew
4. Blankety Blank
5. Home and Away
6. The X-Files
7. Dawn French
8. 24
9. I'll Be There for You
10. Gary Lineker
11. 1985
12. Holby City

Target Words (1 letter)

LEGISLATE, agile, aisle, elite, gait, gill, gilt, gist, isle, islet, legalist, legit, lilt, list, sail, siege, sill, silt, site, slit, stile, still, tail, tile, till, tillage

Target Words (2 letter)

SCRATCHED, cash, cashed, chase, chased, chest, crash, crashed, dash, rash, scratch, search, shade, share, shear, shed, shred

---

Jack's Pub Quiz – History

1. Dallas
2. Charles de Gaulle
3. Pompeii
4. Yuri Gagarin
5. Rome
6. 1912
7. Richard Nixon
8. Nicholas II
9. Israel
10. 1916
11. Richard I
12. 1605

Andy's Pigeon Peril

Andy's CrossWord

Across: 1 Ethos, 4 Bar graphs, 9 Incisor, 10 Pop star, 11 Unarm, 13 Lolly, 15 May, 16 Eve, 17 Latin, 19 El Cid, 21 Nylon, 23 Adder, 24 Jus, 25 Bra, 26 Magma, 28 Toner, 29 Amharic, 31 Ireland, 33 Scrutable, 34 Egypt.

Down: 1 Epicurean, 2 Hectare, 3 S A S, 4 Beryl, 5 Rip, 6 Reply, 7 Potomac, 8 Stray, 12 Melon, 14 Lined, 18 Twang, 19 Egret, 20 Discredit, 22 Leather, 24 January, 25 Bears, 26 Merit, 27 Alike, 30 Cob, 32 Eye.

Themed word is CHALKIE

Jack's Pub Quiz – Sports

1. Horseracing
2. Darts
3. Extras
4. Cardiff City (in 1927)
5. Greyhound racing (dogs' trap colours)
6. Lock
7. Sunderland
8. St Andrews
9. 22 (15 reds + yellow, green, brown, blue, pink, black….and the cue ball!
10. They have all been manager of England's football team
11. 2012
12. Fred Perry

Don't Cop It

Jack's Pub Quiz – Movie Special

1. C-3PO
2. Spanish
3. Vinnie Jones
4. Harry Potter
5. Italian
6. Quentin Tarantino
7. Prince Charming
8. French
9. Finding Forrester
10. Alfred the Butler
11. Ethan Hunt
12. Elliott Gould
13. He played a woman, Tracy's mother
14. Jane Seymour
15. Hugh Grant
16. Jodie Foster
17. Danny DeVito
18. Jennifer Aniston
19. Tommy Lee Jones
20. Robert Pattinson
21. Liam Neeson
22. Ron Weasley
23. Julie Andrews
24. Slumdog Milliionaire
25. Brad Pitt

Andy's CrossWord

Across: 7 Discrete, 9 Abroad, 10 Fete, 11 Expression, 12 Isobar, 14 Inundate, 15 Sample, 16 Fervid, 19 Break out, 21 Ensign, 23 Dead weight, 24 Half, 25 Unveil, 26 Apoplexy.

Down: 1 Miners, 2 G C S E, 3 Cerebral, 4 Gateau, 5 Crash dives, 6 Cavorted, 8 Esprit, 13 Bombardier, 15 Sergeant, 17 Electron, 18 Stigma, 20 Openly, 22 Galaxy, 24 Halo.

Themed word is PERCY

PAGE 103.

Jack's Pub Quiz - General Knowledge

1. Seven - red, orange, yellow, green, blue, indigo and violet
2. Birmingham
3. Duke of Edinburgh
4. EastEnders
5. Badger
6. Ben Nevis
7. Apples
8. John Wayne
9. 1979
10. Jordan
11. The London Eye
12. One Direction

PAGE 115.

THE WORD OF CAPP

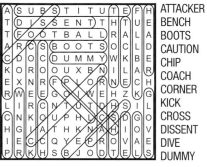

```
A S U B S T I T U T E F H
T D I S S E N T H T U E
T F O O T B A L L R A A
A R C S B O O T S O C D
C D O C D U M M Y K K E
K O R O O U X B N W K R
E X N R F P L O R I N H
R W E E G O W E H Z E G
L I R C N T U T H S K L
C N K O U P H L S S D O
H G A T H K N A H I I V
I E C Q Y E P R O C O E
P R K H S B J O D E T L S
```

ATTACKER
BENCH
BOOTS
CAUTION
CHIP
COACH
CORNER
KICK
CROSS
DISSENT
DIVE
DUMMY

FOOTBALL · HEADER · SHOT
FOUL · PASS · SUBSTITUTE
FULL BACK · PITCH · TACKLE
GLOVES · RED CARD · THROW-IN
GOAL · SCORE · WINGER

PAGE 127.

Jack's Pub Quiz - Transport

1. The Mini
2. Harley-Davidson
3. Heathrow
4. Tandem
5. Porsche
6. Routemaster
7. Submarine
8. Two Fat Ladies
9. Reliant
10. 1976
11. A steam locomotive (which still holds the world speed record for a steam locomotive)
12. Motorcycling

PAGE 132.

Roll out the barrel

PAGE 136 AND 137.

Guitar Bob's Missing Lyrics Quiz

	SONG	Missing lyrics
1.	Waterloo	Couldn't **escape if I** wanted to
2.	Like a Virgin	Touched for the very **first time**
3.	Summer Nights	He showed off **splashing around**
4.	Delilah	**So before they** come to break down the door
5.	Hey Jude	**Don't carry the world** upon your shoulders
6.	Sweet Caroline	Will it fill up with **only two**
7.	American Pie	Drove **my Chevy** to the levee, but the levee was dry
8.	Brown Eyed Girl	Skipping and **a jumping**
9.	Bohemian Rhapsody	I'm just a poor boy, **I need no sympathy**
10.	Don't Stop Believin'	Some were born to **sing the blues**
11.	Livin' on a Prayer	**Take my hand** and we'll make it – I swear
12.	Beat it	No one wants to be **defeated**
13.	Roar	I got the **eye of the tiger**
14.	I Walk the Line	I keep a **close watch** on this heart of mine
15.	The Wonder of You	You give me hope **and consolation**
16.	Price Tag	We just wanna make **the world dance**
17.	Earth Song	What about sunrise, **what about rain**
18.	Back for Good	Whatever I said, whatever **I did, I didn't mean it**
19.	Rotterdam	This could be Rotterdam **or anywhere**
20.	Bermuda Triangle	Bermuda Triangle, it makes people **disappear**
21.	Umbrella	When the sun shines, we'll **shine together**
22.	Space Oddity	**Ground control** to Major Tom
23.	Ebony and Ivory	Ebony and Ivory, live together in **perfect harmony**
24.	Venus	I'm your Venus, I'm your fire, at **your desire**
25.	Careless Whisper	**Guilty feet** have got no rhythm

PAGE 139.

THE WORD OF CAPP

```
B O O K M A K E R S T
J S Q W S T L E G E R
K T U B N Y V F R P I
S A R Q B E T O A P P
T K J R O J R D D E L
A E E I A J D I D D E
R D G W K D I S S O C
T E M D S T N M T C K
F G U A E D E Q A A O
S T A L L S R M N J W
S T A B L E L A D M N
```

BOOKMAKERS
DERBY
GRANDSTAND
OAKS
ODDS
OWNER
PADDOCK
ST LEGER

STABLE LAD
STAKE
STALLS
START
STUD
TRAINER
TRIPLE CROWN

PAGE 154 AND 155.

Jack's Pub Quiz - Festive Bumper

1. Rook
2. Ringo Starr
3. Florin (or two bob bit)
4. Green
5. The Six Million Dollar Man
6. Gordon Brown
7. They are all locations for major theme parks
8. Robin Hood
9. Irish
10. Ford
11. Tay
12. 19
13. Dover
14. The Oaks
15. Jeremy Clarkson
16. Blockbusters
17. India Pale Ale
18. Scottish
19. Ian Fleming (author of the James Bond books)
20. Blackpool
21. Bicycle
22. Pewter
23. Carlsberg
24. Six – red, yellow, green, blue, orange, white
25. Lady Gaga

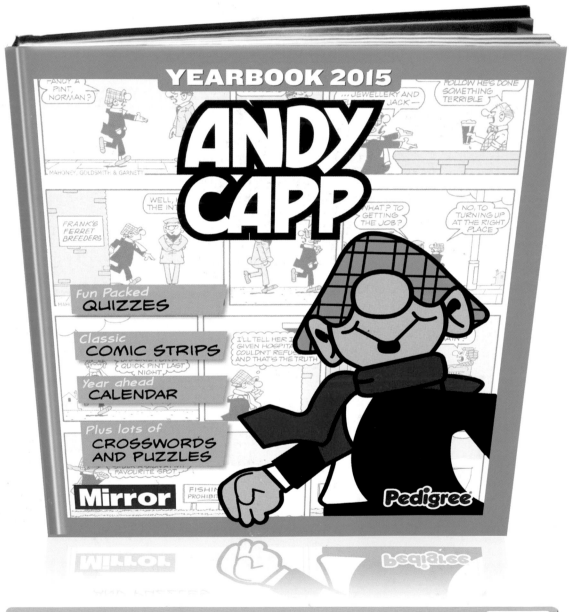